EXISTENTIAL PROGRAM MANUAL

WALDO VIEIRA, M.D.

EXISTENTIAL PROGRAM MANUAL

Translator: Kevin de La Tour
Editor: Simone de La Tour
Proofreaders: Álvaro Salgado
Pamela Hughes

RIO DE JANEIRO, RJ - BRAZIL

INTERNATIONAL INSTITUTE OF PROJECTIOLOGY
AND CONSCIENTIOLOGY

1997

First Edition in English – 1997 – 2,000 copies

Copyright © 1997 by Waldo Vieira

All rights reserved. No part of this book may be reproduced or transmitted in any form or by any means, electronic or mechanical, including photocopying, recording, or by any information storage and retrieval system, without permission in writing from the author.

Notes: - The author's rights to this edition have been graciously transferred by the author to the International Institute of Projectiology and Conscientiology (IIPC).

- The original pages of this edition were produced and revised using electronic desktop publishing and laser printing (text in Times New Roman; 218.157 characters; 34.284 words; 6.220 lines and 2.089 paragraphs).

- We would like to thank Mr. A.S. for all the help received during the publication of this book.

Printing and binding: OESP Gráfica S.A.
Cover: Fernando Alberto Santos
Photo: Geysa Adnet

Card Catalog information prepared by the International Institute of Projectiology and Conscientiology (IIPC) Center of Information and Documentation

Vieira, Waldo, 1932 -

V658e Existential Program Manual / Waldo Vieira. - 1st Edition in English – Rio de Janeiro: International Institute of Projectiology and Conscientiology, 1997.
182 p.

1. Conscientiology. 2. Projectiology. I. Title

ISBN 85-86019-18-6   CDD 133

International Institute of Projectiology and Conscientiology (IIPC)
R. Visconde de Pirajá, 572 / 6° andar - Ipanema - Rio de Janeiro - RJ - Brazil - CEP 22410-002 – Tel.: 55-21-512-9229 – Fax: 55-21-512-4735
Caixa Postal 70.000 - CEP 22422-970
Internet: E-mail – iipc@ax.ibase.org.br
Home Page – http://www.iipc.org.br

TO THE READER:

Conscientiology. Conscientiology (the formal study of consciousness) indicates, with rationality and logic, 2 priority concepts for us all:

1. **Object.** Your multi-dimensional consciousness (personality, intelligent principle), when lucid, is the first and most important *object* for you to *research,* both theoretically and practically.

2. **Objective.** The comprehensive execution of *your* human *life's programming* is the first and most important *objective* for you to *accomplish* in theory and practice.

The Author

Existential Program Manual

TABLE OF CONTENTS

To the Reader 5

1. The Existential Program (I) 9
2. Categories of Existential Program 12
3. Existential Mini-program (II) 14
4. Existential Maxi-program (III) 17
5. Rational Laws of the Existential Program 20
6. Existential Program Test 23
7. Identification of Personal Existential Program 26
8. Personal Traits Formula (I) 29
9. Personal Reciprocation Formula (II) 31
10. Characteristics of the Consolation Task (I) 33
11. Characteristics of the Clarification Task (II) 35
12. Instruments for Executing the Existential Program 38
13. Macro-somatics 49
14. Existential Program and Geography 52
15. Existential Program Execution Technique (I) 55
16. The *"Is Still Not"* Technique (II) 59
17. Existential Anti-program 61
18. Existential Program and Consciential Ectopia 72
19. Ideological Dissidence (I) 76
20. Existential Program and Mini-dissidence (II) 81

21. Consciential Tri-endowment 84
22. Intellectuality in the Existential Program (I) 87
23. Mentalsomatics 93
24. Psychic Capacities in the Existential Program (II) 95
25. Consciential Energies 98
26. Communicability in the Existential Program (III) 102
27. Communicative Projectability 104
28. Existential Program and Time 106
29. Short-term Accomplishments (I) 112
30. Mid-term Accomplishments (II) 113
31. Long-term Accomplishments (III) 114
32. Existential Completism (I) 116
33. Existential Incompletism (II) 121
34. Existential Multi-completism (III) 126
35. Existential Moratorium (I) 128
36. Existential Mini-moratorium (II) 129
37. Existential Maxi-moratorium (III) 130
38. Evolutionary Pre-requisites 133
39. Minimums and Maximums 135
40. Permanent-total-freedom-from-intrusion 138

Glossary of Conscientiology 140

Bibliography 165

Index 167

1. THE EXISTENTIAL PROGRAM

Definition. The personal *existential program* is the specific programming of each intraphysical consciousness (human personality – see glossary) in his or her new life in this human dimension, that is planned before the somatic (physical) rebirth of consciousness, while still an extraphysical consciousness (non-physical personality).

Synonymy. The following 9 expressions are used to characterize the existential program:

1. *Existential goal.*
2. *Existential orientation.*
3. *Existential planning.*
4. *Existential project.*
5. *Intraphysical objective.*
6. *Intraphysical task.*
7. *Life project.*
8. *Pre-intraphysical mandate.*
9. *Terrestrial mission.*

THE EXISTENTIAL PROGRAM IS THE OBJECT OF STUDY IN EXISTENTIAL PROGRAMOLOGY, A SPECIALTY OF CONSCIENTIOLOGY.

Sub-specialties. Existential programology studies, among others, the following 17 sub-specialties: the binomial abnegation - existential moratorium, consciential abstentionism, consciential ectopia, consciential gestation, existential completism, existential incompletism, existential maxi-moratorium, existential maxi-program, existential mini-moratorium, existential mini-program, existential moratorium, existential multi-completism, existential program, pre-intraphysical mandate, theorice (theory + practice), the trinomial existential program - existential completism - existential moratorium, the trinomial motivation-effort-perseverance (see glossary).

THE CONSCIOUS EXISTENTIAL PROGRAM IS STILL A CONDITION ACHIEVED BY A SMALL MINORITY OF HUMANITY.

Destiny. The basic destiny – fundamental directives – of the intraphysical consciousness' life come already written in his or her biological, genetic and para-genetic (non-physical genetic) origins including, in this context, the intermissive course (preparation between two physical lives), innate ideas and existential program. The details of human life nevertheless change all the time.

Determinism. The determinism in our life is basic but relative.

Freedom. Our conditional freedom of consciential manifestation is always much greater than we think it is.

Variation. We are all born knowing many things – paragenetics and innate ideas – but the nature of our knowledge, experiences and the degree of evolutionary quality within the parameters of the existential program's experiences vary greatly.

Evolutionology. From the evolutionary condition of the pre-serenissimus (serenissimus is a consciousness who is about to end his or her cycle of physical rebirths) of today – common to all intraphysical consciousnesses who breathe on Earth – to the condition of the evolutionologist, or the Evolutionary Orientor (extraphysical consciousness who coordinates existential programs), we will attain the permanently-totally-intrusion-free condition (intrusion is a negative influence by another consciousness). In this way we achieve a certain level of versatility in terms of our consciential talents and attributes.

Contract. Nonetheless, no one arrives in intraphysical life with an envelope in hand containing the details of the contract to be completed in the current existence.

Order. No one receives a written proscribed order, after a few decades of intraphysical life, regarding that which they came here to do.

The greatest astuteness with regards to the existential program is to know how to employ various consciential attributes at the same time in intraphysical life.

Mega-fraternity. The more advanced or evolved an existential program, the greater is the degree of practiced mega-fraternity included in the planning of the intermissive course.

Objective. Regardless of your existential program, your objective will always be to become permanently-totally-intrusion-free, if you have not already reached this status.

Permanently-totally-intrusion-free. It is important to consider that the condition of being permanently-totally-intrusion-free can be achieved in only one human lifetime.

Period. The intelligent thing to do is to take advantage of the period of *acceleration* in which we are living, wherein modern civilization is offering greater evolutionary possibilities to the human personality than ever before.

2. CATEGORIES OF EXISTENTIAL PROGRAM

THE EXECUTION OF AN EXISTENTIAL PROGRAM IS THE THEORETICAL AND PRACTICAL RESULT OF A HUMAN CONSCIOUSNESS' PRIORITIZATIONS.

Categories. There are diverse categories of existential programs. They are shaped by the nature, scope and other qualifications of thosenic realizations (thosene = thought + sentiment/emotion + energy) that are required of the intraphysical consciousness. The following are 6 categories.

1. **Holo-karmality.** In terms of holo-karma (holo-karma = the 3 types of karma when considered as a whole), there are 3 categories of existential program:
A. **Ego-karmic.** The existential program that is excessively *personal*, being influenced by the ego, or the "belly-brain" (see glossary) or infantile egocentrism and its consequences.
B. **Group-karmic.** The *groupal existential program*, or that restricted to one's primary or secondary karmic group or other families or evolutionary groupings.
C. **Poly-karmic.** The more evolved *poly-karmic existential program* of non-remunerated work that is performed in solidarity towards others within the scope of mega-fraternity. It is always related to an existential maxi-program.

2. **Intermissivity.** In regards to the intermissive course, there are 2 categories of existential program:
A. **Technical.** With the intermissive course recalled and applied through one's acts.
B. **Instinctive.** Without an intermissive course developed in one's most recent intermissive period.

3. **Evolutionality.** In regards to one's evolutionary level, 4 levels of existential programs exist for men and women:

    A. **Vulgar.** That of the vulgar pre-serenissimus or *Homo sapiens*.

    B. **Permanently-totally-intrusion-free.** That of the pre-serenissimus who has achieved the permanently-totally-intrusion-free condition.

    C. **Evolutionologist.** That of the evolutionologist or evolutionary orientor (see glossary).

    D. **Serenissimus.** That of serenissimus or *Homo sapiens serenissimus*.

4. **Universality.** In terms of the scope of the intraphysical consciousness' manifestations, there are 2 categories of existential program:

    A. **Individual.** The intraphysical consciousness when considered individually, in the category of ego-karma.

    B. **Groupal.** The intraphysical consciousness when considered groupally, in the categories of group-karma and poly-karma.

5. **Authenticity.** Regarding authenticity in its execution, there are 2 categories of existential program:

    A. **Secret.** The existential program carried out diplomatically, or in secret.

    B. **Explicit.** The existential program carried out explicitly or frankly.

IN TERMS OF EVOLUTIONARY SCOPE, THERE ARE 2 BASIC CATEGORIES OF EXISTENTIAL PROGRAM: THE EXISTENTIAL MINI-PROGRAM AND THE EXISTENTIAL MAXI-PROGRAM.

3. EXISTENTIAL MINI-PROGRAM

Definition. The *existential mini-program* is a minimal, smaller, elementary, "retail" existential program. It is receptive in nature (oriented towards personal gain) and is dedicated to specifically individual (ego-karmic) issues within one's karmic group. It is obviously a lesser evolutionary task.

Synonymy. The following 7 expressions illustrate some different types of existential mini-programs:

A. *Ego-karmic existential program.*
B. *Elementary existential program.*
C. *Infantile existential program.*
D. *Lesser existential program.*
E. *Receptive existential program.*
F. *Restricted existential program.*
G. *Retail existential program.*

Priorities. In existential mini-programs, intentionality and personal effort will more commonly convey the now physically mature individual towards the gradual implantation of priority tasks without traumatic mutations or *evolutionary rapes.*

THOSE WHO ARE UNAWARE OF THE EXISTENTIAL PROGRAM HAVE OBVIOUSLY ONLY BEEN ASSIGNED AN EGO-KARMIC EXISTENTIAL MINI-PROGRAM.

Competitiveness. In evolutionary endeavors, it is worthwhile to compete with oneself, thus allowing a greater efficiency in the execution of one's evolutionary program and better ideas on a day-to-day basis.

Collections. All of us have work to accomplish on this planet. No one comes to this intraphysical dimension only to collect ties or antique cars. Neither does one come to play all the time.

Children. In general, children are still living in the beginning of the *preparatory* phase of the existential program. The majority of existential completisms (completion of an existential program) occur only in the *execution* phase of existential programs.

THERE ARE EXISTENTIAL MINI-PROGRAMS THAT ARE RELATIVE TO THE INTRAPHYSICAL LIFETIME *THAT IS SPECIFIC TO A CHILD.*

Apparition. No consciousness dies. The parents or guardians of a small child who passed through de-soma (biological death) at a tender age, and are not guilty of causing this de-soma, witness some type of apparition of that child's extraphysical consciousness.

De-soma. The apparition, according to research, occurs within the first 12 months after the child's first de-soma (biological death) when, in the condition of an extraphysical consciousness, they have passed through the second de-soma (discarding of the dense, animal energies of one's holochakra or energy body).

Extraphysical euphoria. This fact is evidence that the child's *existential mini-program (relative to time)* was completed and that he or she, now an extraphysical consciousness, is enjoying an extraphysical euphoria and wants to comfort and alleviate his or her ex-parents or ex-guardians, sharing his or her well-being and happiness (extraphysical euphoria) with them.

Abstensionism. Consciential abstentionism is the indifference, negligence, distancing from or a position of neutrality of an intraphysical consciousness in reference to his or her integrated maturity (holomaturity*)* and conscious evolution.

Existential programology. Consciential abstentionism directly affects the execution of the intraphysical consciousness' existential program, which is, for this reason, being studied in existential programology.

Groupality. As a result of social mimicry (repetition of social behavior), consciential abstentionism can extend its paralyzing influence to a small social group, completely nullifying an entire team project and even groupal existential programs.

Self-mimicry. Unnecessary self-mimicry (repetition of personal behavior from past lives), due to self-disorganization or an absence of evolutionary continuism, is the major cause of personal existential incompletism (failure to complete one's existential program) and, as a secondary effect, even groupal existential incompletism (group-mimicry).

UP TO A CERTAIN POINT, CONSCIENTIAL ABSTENTIONISM IS A TYPE OF SITTING-ON-THE-FENCE IN THIS STILL PATHOLOGICAL INTRAPHYSICAL SOCIETY.

4. EXISTENTIAL MAXI-PROGRAM

Definition. The *existential maxi-program* is a greater, advanced, altruistic, maximal existential program having a *wholesale* approach, that is consciously dedicated to the collective good.

Synonymy. These 6 expressions characterize the existential maxi-program:

A. *Advanced existential program.*
B. *Altruistic existential program.*
C. *Ample existential program.*
D. *Existential mega-program.*
E. *Greater existential program.*
F. *Poly-karmic existential program.*
G. *Wholesale existential program.*

Leadership. The existential maxi-program is that of the *evolutionary-leader-intraphysical-consciousness*, who is operating within a specific, more universalistic and maxi-fraternal group-karmic libertarian task.

Mini-piece. In a unified, altruistic assistential task, the intraphysical consciousness represents a lucid, active human mini-piece (cog) within the maxi-mechanism of the multi-dimensional team.

The existential maxi-program is an alternative intraphysical destiny, different from the existence of the common intraphysical consciousness belonging to the unthinking masses.

Poly-karmality. Poly-karmality, which goes beyond ego-karmality and group-karmality, inevitably enters into the execution of the existential maxi-program, and is characterized by performance of the clarification task.

Truths. Strictly speaking, the clarification task is the living of one's life according to relative leading-edge truths in favor of humanity and para-humanity.

Groupality. Groupality is the condition of evolution in group, or the quality of a consciousness' (intraphysical or extraphysical consciousness) evolutionary group (group-karma).

Groupal. Existential maxi-programs direct the individual towards groupal existential programs or existential programs executed by more than one intraphysical consciousness, established through cosmoethical consciential ties.

ONLY THOSE WHO NO LONGER ASK FOR THEMSELVES *ARE ASSIGNED TO EXECUTE EXISTENTIAL MAXI-PROGRAMS (AMPLE SENSE).*

Sex-love. Just as the exercising of mature sexuality is neither sick, painful, disagreeable, sinful, prohibited, sordid nor dirty; the experience of romantic love is neither absurd, abnormal, disastrous, fantastical, insane, obsessing nor foolish.

Love. Pure romantic love is action, certainty, completeness, healthy complicity, paradise, pleasure, prodigality, wealth, tenderness and the ennoblement of the existential maxi-program.

Code. The *Personal Cosmoethical Code* is a relevant creation for the intraphysical consciousness' evolution and the preparation for the execution of a greater existential program.

Prevention. This Code functions as an evolutionary prevention, vaccinating the individual against obstinacy or insistence in repeating those same age-old errors that we bring from the past.

Incorruptibility. When an intraphysical consciousness identifies his or her patho-thosenes, *little venial sins* and self-corruptions, they are actually seeking the attainable status of personal incorruptibility.

Exam. In advanced intermissive courses, there are evolutionary work boards that make selections using a type of entrance exam that is administered by the evolutionologists.

Extraphysical consciousnesses. These admission exams were created for the selection of the extraphysical consciousnesses who are more apt for the performance of *specific existential programs* on Earth.

Candidates. Dozens of extraphysical consciousnesses apply for participation in these entrance exams, accepting the condition of being future mini-pieces (cogs) operating within a maxi-mechanism of interconsciential assistance.

Demands. Certain existential maxi-programs may require a macro-soma (customized physical body), ideological maxi-dissidence, consciential tri-endowments, the condition of being a consciential epicenter (core of energetic support), existential multi-completism, existential maxi-moratorium (extension of physical life for execution of further tasks), or even the permanently-totally-intrusion-free condition.

Sumo. For example: would a traditional *(sumotori)* practitioner of sumo (ancestral career) need hundreds of years of *multi-existential recycling* through continuous self-relays (see glossary) in order to get away from his *existential* mini-programs and achieve an existential maxi-program?

THE HELPERS ASSIST IN THE MORE UNIVERSAL EXISTENTIAL MAXI-PROGRAMS AS EMISSARIES OF THE EVOLUTIONARY ORIENTORS.

Existential mega-program. Not rarely, the details of an existential program are complex. An intraphysical consciousness can live a physical life without any kind of religion or reading volume upon volume of mystical works and nevertheless be the completist of an existential mega-program.

Evolution. The more evolved an intraphysical consciousness is, the greater his or her capacity will be to perform an existential program. However, the existential program will become increasingly sophisticated and difficult to complete compared to the vulgar intraphysical consciousness' existential program.

5. RATIONAL LAWS OF THE EXISTENTIAL PROGRAM

THE EXISTENTIAL PROGRAM *IS REALIZED IN EVERY MINUTE OF ONE'S EXISTENCE, AS A RESULT OF LITTLE, GREAT THINGS.*

Principles. The essential premises or principles of more lucid *consciousnesses'* life programs on Earth obey logical, just directives that can be characterized as being rational laws of the *existential program*. The following 14 examples are given in alphabetical order:

1. **Adaptability.** The *existential program* is adaptable or changeable, being susceptible to renovations or amplifications, according to the complexity of its development and the extension of the *consciential* or *intraphysical* universe that comprises its tasks. Evolution signifies mutability and renovation.

2. **Assistentiality.** The executor of an *existential program* is the first *consciousness* to be assisted or to benefit from it. Any *existential program* coming from an *evolutionologist* constitutes a good evolutionary endeavor.

3. **Compatibility.** Every *existential program* is compatible with a *consciousness'* temperament and is suited to the evolutionary level of his or her multi-millenary experiential background.

4. **Conscientiality.** The *extraphysical consciousness'* level of *conscientiality*, *holo-karmic net-balance* or evolutionary file determine the degree of lucidity regarding the directives of his or her *existential program* while in the condition of an *intraphysical consciousness*.

5. **Cosmoethicality.** Every existential program is fundamentally *cosmoethical* in its premises and aims. The orientations coming from an *evolutionologist* are essentially *cosmoethical*.

6. **Ego-karmality.** Even when based in *poly-karmality*, every *existential program* first attends to the *ego-karmality* of the *consciousness*.

7. **Evolutionality.** The *existential program* depends on the evolutionary level or personal merit of the *extraphysical consciousness*. Evidently, not all *consciousnesses* receive an *existential program* in which every minute detail is planned in advance.

8. **Exclusivity.** Every *existential program* is unique, singular, personalized or exclusive to a determinate *consciousness*.

THERE DOES NOT EXIST 2 CONSCIOUSNESSES *WHO RECEIVE 2 IDENTICAL* EXISTENTIAL PROGRAMS – *NOT EVEN SIAMESE TWINS.*

9. **Executability.** Every *existential program* is fully capable of being executed with a reasonable amount of latitude being allowed for, within the *intraphysical consciousness'* evolutionary context and given his or her level of competence. The agenda of an *existential program* may be complex and problematic, but never unrealizable. The layout of an *existential program* obviously does not contain unjust or unjustifiable clauses.

10. **Group-karmality.** Each *existential program* receives some direct or indirect orientation from the *evolutionologist* or *evolutionary orientor* of the *karmic group*. Every evolutionary group has hundreds of *evolutionologists*.

11. **Interactivity.** *Existential programs* are not mutually exclusive. No *existential program* requires that another one be eliminated in order for it to be concluded.

12. **Intercooperativity.** Existential programs, although extremely personal are, paradoxically, interdependent to a degree and not competitive. Quite to the contrary, they are intercooperative.

13. **Nontransferability.** Every *existential program* is personalized and nontransferable, being specifically tailored to a certain *consciousness*. All substitution of tasks, in the evolutionary echelons of *consciousnesses*, adheres to this principle.

14. **Uniqueness.** *Existential programs* are unique in their structural directives. Two *existential programs* may be similar, but will never be identical in regards to their scope and objectives. No 2 *consciousnesses* are identical.

EVERY EXISTENTIAL PROGRAM FIRST ADDRESSES THE EVOLUTION OF THE INTRAPHYSICAL CONSCIOUSNESS PER SE, EVEN WHEN OPERATING WITHIN GROUP-KARMA.

6. EXISTENTIAL PROGRAM TEST

EVERY EXISTENTIAL PROGRAM DEMANDS DAILY CULTIVATION, BASED ON ONE NATURAL FACT: NOT EVERY SEED GERMINATES.

Test. Chapter 549 of the book *"700 Conscientiology Experiments"* is a test on the *existential program* that is presented here in its general form in order to clarify the subject.

Contrasts. Following are 30 contrasts, listed in order to allow you to identify the differences between an *advanced existential program* (first echelon) and an *elementary existential program* (second echelon):

    1. High recuperation of personal *cons* (units of consciousness).
       Low recuperation of *cons*.
    2. High valuation of human time.
       Low valuation of human time.
    3. Lucid *consciential wholesale approach*.
       Vulgar *consciential retail approach*.
    4. Minimum indispensable self-mimicry.
       Dispensable self-mimicry.
    5. Cosmic *conscientiality*.
       Tropospheric *conscientiality*.
    6. *Cosmoethical conscientiality*.
       Anti-cosmoethical *conscientiality*.
    7. *Intraphysical consciousness* operating from the *head-brain*.
       Intraphysical consciousness operating from the *belly-brain*.
    8. *Intraphysical consciousness* who is part of an active *evolutionary duo*.

Intraphysical consciousness not a part of an *evolutionary duo*.
9. An already lucid universalist *intraphysical consciousness*.
A still vulgar sectarian *intraphysical consciousness*.
10. An advanced *intermissive course*.
An obviously elementary *intermissive course*.
11. Non-conformist spirit (neophile).
More conformist spirit (neophobe).
12. *Holochakral* flexibility (CEs or consciential energies).
Holochakral inflexibility (CEs).
13. More multi-dimensional interests.
More intraphysical interests.
14. Invests more in one's own *existential program*.
Invests less in one's own *existential program*.
15. Liberation from one's *consciential basement* (egocentric instinctive behavior).
Adult imprisonment in one's *consciential basement*.
16. Greater degree of freedom from one's *group-karma*.
Distinct *group-karmic inter-prison*.
17. Greater *holosomatic homeostasis* (balanced state of all bodies).
Lesser *holosomatic homeostasis*.
18. Elevated level of conscious prioritization.
Low level of conscious prioritization.
19. Conscious *poly-karmic* objectives.
Vulgar *group-karmic* objectives.

WE CAN NOT DEMAND ADVANCED PERFORMANCE *FROM THOSE WHO HAVE AN ELEMENTARY* EXISTENTIAL PROGRAM *TO EXECUTE.*

20. *Thosenity* (consideration of thosenes (thoughts + sentiments/emotions + energy)) with an emphasis on *tho* (thought).
Thosenity with an emphasis on *sen* (sentiments/emotions).
21. Carrier of healthy retrocognitions.

Carrier of pathological retrocognitions.
22. Vanguard position in one's karmic group.
Vulgar position in one's karmic group.
23. Predominance of *strong* traits in personal conduct.
Predominance of *weak* traits in personal conduct.
24. Conscious (lucid) projectability (ability to project one's consciousness) (LP).
Still unconscious projectability.
25. Effector of existential inversion (technique for youths to optimize consciential performance) and an existential *maxi-program*.
Realizer merely of existential recycling.
26. Self-scrutinized holochakral seduction.
Sexo-chakral seduction without self-scrutiny.
27. Adherent to consciential paradigm.
Adherent to conventional paradigm.
28. More rare outbursts of immaturity.
More frequent outbursts of immaturity.
29. Works towards clarification.
Works towards elementary consolation.
30. Evident consciential tri-endowment.
Vulgar consciential mono-endowment.

Question. Are you aware of the intrinsic reality of your existential program? What is the exact type of your existential program?

Theorical. The correct execution of the existential program is a theorical (theoretical + practical) result of the intraphysical consciousness' prioritizations.

7. IDENTIFICATION OF PERSONAL EXISTENTIAL PROGRAM

Questions. The following are some questions that are opportune and extremely appropriate for everyone to ask themselves:

A. Self-awareness. Am I aware of my existential program?
B. Indications. Have I already encountered any indications as to what my existential program is in this life?
C. Presupposition. What is my presupposed existential program?
D. Preparation. Am I on the path of my existential program?

Assistentiality. The more advanced one's intermissive course is, the greater the degree of concomitant interconsciential assistance that is executed by the extraphysical consciousness in preparation for the upcoming intraphysical life, or rather, during the planning of his or her existential program.

MILLIONS OF INDIVIDUALS ALL OVER THE EARTH FEEL THEY HAVE SOMETHING TO ACCOMPLISH IN INTRAPHYSICAL LIFE.

Evolutionologist. No evolutionologist or extraphysical existential programmer recommends an existential program without having the certainty that it can be completed very well, according to the evolutionary caliber and potentialities of that consciousness for whom it is prepared.

Limits. The entire planning of existential programs is objectively proposed to the extraphysical consciousness who is a candidate for re-soma (rebirth), according to his or her limitations and endurance, given his or her evolutionary experiences.

Justifications. The plans of an existential program do not allow unbecoming justifications, excuses or any type of self-corruption in terms of its completion in the near future.

Marginality. On the other hand, no evolutionologist plans an existential program – which is always cosmoethical – in order for someone to come to physical life and be a drug dealer, a criminal or antisocial being, belong to the Mafias of pathological intraphysical society, or to take the life of another person.

Crimes. No famous crime or assassination of an eminent personality, or even an unknown individual, was induced through the planning of the existential program.

Suicide. The clauses established in an existential program or the demands related to its execution are never planned to induce anyone to commit suicide, the apex of pathological, intraphysical self-disorganization.

WE CANNOT FORGET THAT THE LAYOUT OF AN EXISTENTIAL PROGRAM IS STIPULATED IN ACCORDANCE WITH A *CONSCIOUSNESS'* EVOLUTIONARY ENDURANCE.

Intraphysical melancholy. Nevertheless, intraphysical melancholy can pathologically predispose the intraphysical consciousness towards the path of self-destruction – one of the worst and fundamental failures of intraphysical life.

Children. In general, children are still living in the beginning of the *preparatory phase* of the existential program. The majority of existential completisms are only effected in the *execution period* of the existential program.

Factors. When executing a positive *extraphysical* task of an existential program, the following 3 relevant factors influence the intraphysical consciousness, in decreasing order of importance:

1. **Health.** The condition of maintained personal health.

2. **Self-discipline.** The habits of constant self-discipline.

3. **Money.** Available money, or relative personal financial security.

Intraphysical consciousness. Based on these and other factors, the day arrives when the intraphysical consciousness wants to know what they came to do in this world and sets off in search of the identification and the correct direction of his or her existential program.

Technique. The technique for identification of one's personal existential program is always more effective when developed through basic, logical self-scrutinizing formulas of intraphysical ledgers or consciential self-evaluation.

ONE CAN IDENTIFY ONE'S EXISTENTIAL PROGRAM USING 2 FORMULAS: THAT OF PERSONAL TRAITS AND OF PERSONAL RECIPROCATION.

8. PERSONAL TRAITS FORMULA

Strong traits. *First formula:* on a sheet of paper, in 2 columns, establish a comparison between your *strong traits*, or talents, virtues and capacities, in the left column; and your *weak traits*, or defects, bad habits and vices, in the right column.

Balance. Upon comparison, the net-balance of the potentialities that you have demonstrated up to the present in this human life is obtained.

Hetero-scrutiny. When it is difficult to make this comparison, it is better to give a sheet of paper to every person who is close to you, or in your social circle.

Request. This paper must include a completely sincere request for each one to write down criticisms of us, or what they think of our talents and defects, with the intention of improving our evolutionary conduct.

Computer. After this, if possible, the ideal would be to put the common denominators, or the repeating commentaries, into a computer, highlighting the percentages of the facets that are more evident about our personality.

THE BEST INDIVIDUALS FOR SUPPLYING INDICATIONS REGARDING OUR SELF-CORRUPTIONS ARE THOSE WHO WE CONSIDER TO BE PROBLEMATIC.

Explicit. Those who have conflicts with us or have raised questions with us regarding our points of view, ideas, affectivities or individual and group actions, will be more explicit in their criticisms.

Conscientiogram. The individual who is a more interested researcher can, in terms of applying this first formula, employ the more sophisticated resources of the conscientiogram.

Conscientiometry. The conscientiogram is a technical agenda for making advanced evaluative measurements of a consciousness' evolutionary level, a fundamental part of conscientiometry.

Self-knowledge. Upon knowing ourselves better, we can accelerate our evolutionary conquests by distinguishing which personal points we need to work on and being able to utilize our own attributes.

Scars. Personal experiences first create abrasions and then scars in our consciential micro-universe (personal world).

Para-genetics. These scars compose, little by little, over many millenniums, our extremely unique para-genetics.

THE MORE EXPERIENCED AND EVOLVED CONSCIOUSNESS IS THE ONE EXHIBITING MORE PARA-SCARS IN THE HOLOSOMA.

9. Personal Reciprocation Formula

Key question. In each area of our existential program to be performed, there exists a key question that must be discovered, identified and answered by its executor.

Net-balance. In the net-balance of the existential program, the key question is: "Have I paid back what I have received in the school of Earth?"

Income. Thus the *second formula* arises: with a good amount of self-scrutiny, you establish a comparison between your *intraphysical income,* or all that you have received that is good in your human life in relation to your *personal reciprocation.*

Reciprocation. Personal reciprocation is that which you have directly and personally already given back for the betterment of the realities of the cosmos and its inhabitants.

THE NET-BALANCE BETWEEN WHAT YOU HAVE RECEIVED AND YOUR RECIPROCATION TO LIFE PROVIDES THE DIRECTIVES FOR THE EXECUTION OF YOUR EXISTENTIAL PROGRAM.

Obligations. Upon having your *initial directives*, you will work to improve the programming of your life in light of the 3 following categories of personal evolutionary duties or obligations:

1. **Realizations.** Obligations already accomplished.
2. **Omissions.** The obligations that have been omitted, forgotten, not perceived, or left for later, at the side of the road of human life.
3. **Pending.** Those obligations that are pending or are still to be executed from now on.

Recycling. The execution of any type of existential program requires periodic and continual recyclings or reviews regarding its details.

Tasks. At the current point of your existential self-evaluation, it is important to consider the 2 basic assistential tasks:
    A. **Consolation task.** Personal or groupal elementary consolation task.
    B. **Clarification task.** The personal or groupal more evolved clarification task.

Group-karmality. In group-karmality, a consciousness executing the consolation task gives expecting to get in return.
Poly-karmality. In poly-karmality, a consciousness executing the clarification task gives without expecting to get in return.
Wisdom. The wisdom of conscious solidarity is already a natural reward.
Binomial. In the binomial impulse-calculation, the consolation task is based more on impulse (belly-brain, cardio-chakra, psychosoma), and the clarification task is based more on calculation (rationality, discernment, mentalsoma).

WHICH OF THE 2 BASIC ASSISTENTIAL TASKS PREDOMINATE IN YOUR EXISTENTIAL PROGRAM: THE CONSOLATION TASK OR THE CLARIFICATION TASK ?

10. CHARACTERISTICS OF THE CONSOLATION TASK

IT IS BETTER TO SEE SOMEONE EXECUTING THE CONSOLATION TASK THAN NO FRATERNAL TASK AT ALL.

Characteristics. The service of fraternal consolatory aid of one consciousness in favor of another, or others, presents at least 20 characteristics:

1. *Pleasing.* Compromises, offers palliatives and *pleases* everyone (simple work).
2. *Yes.* Says *yes* much more often than *no*, in all undertakings.
3. **Dependents.** Attends to those who still need to ask much more for themselves all the time.
4. **Hypocrisy.** Tries to cover up problems using sugar-coated postures, infantile parables and euphemisms with those individuals involved in the most diverse types of insincerities and hypocrisies.
5. **Easy.** Presents easy understanding, agreeable execution, and sympathetic performance with tangible, immediate and compensating results in everyday life.
6. **Quantification.** Supports itself through the passivity of the *masses* and listens to public opinion, prioritizing the quantity of proselytism and indoctrination rendered.
7. **Emotionality.** Invariably utilizes individuals' desires, anxieties and feelings or animalized emotional bodies *(belly-brain)*.
8. **Immaturities.** Dedicates itself to the form of things and the appearance of beings, with palliatives and consciential emergencies, and is not selective in choosing the means to its ends.
9. **Absolutism.** Monopolizes the "truth" and employs absolute definitions, exalting mysticism.
10. **Demagogy.** Appeals to religious and political demagogies so that consciousnesses remain anesthetized in a consciential infancy, at a nursery school level of elementary knowledge.

11. **Existential series.** Promotes the theory of existential series but only exalts the extraphysical consciousness to the detriment of the human, who is an intraphysical consciousness, but also a multi-dimensional being.

12. **Inculcation.** Seeks to implant *sanctity* and salvationism, speaking with austerity, puritanisms, moralistic conventionalisms and *sugar-coated belly-brain-washing*.

13. **Illusion.** Lure with the concept of inner reform, but maintains slavery and promotes the illusion that one can achieve definitive self-evolution with only one intraphysical life.

14. **Crutches.** Employs all *psychological crutches* available, without explaining them, combating them, or offering the means by which individuals can liberate themselves from them.

15. **Manipulation.** Rehashes antiquated formulas in a sacramental tone, manipulating the human masses and maintaining them under unconscious psychological dependencies.

16. **Inhibitions.** Maintains individuals as inhibited listeners who do not express their ideas, for fear of not pleasing, and incapable of making continuous libertarian inquiries.

17. **Orthodoxy.** Emphasizes parochial, segregationist sectarianism, basing its actions in *intransigent orthodoxy*, in an egoistic and self-defensive purism.

18. **Numbness.** Makes the *people* constantly *feel much more* and think less, numbed in cults and myths, immaturities, adorations, guru worship and all such stagings.

19. **Competition.** Concerns itself, in an insecure manner, with the endeavor of systematic, professional indoctrination, competing with the power of religions and philosophies.

20. **Dogmatic.** Maintains untouchable taboos, using irrational dogmas and sacralizations.

YOUR WILL, INTENTION AND STRONG TRAITS DETERMINE THE QUALITY OF THE REALIZATION OF YOUR EXISTENTIAL PROGRAM.

11. CHARACTERISTICS OF THE CLARIFICATION TASK

IT IS BETTER TO SEE OUR PARTNER EXECUTING THE CLARIFICATION TASK RATHER THAN THE CONSOLATION TASK.

Characteristics. Fraternal clarifying assistance performed by one consciousness towards others presents, at minimum, the following 20 characteristics:

1. **Complexity.** Always operating in the minority and against the flow, the clarification task elucidates facts, points out errors and offers more definitive evolutionary solutions (complex work).

2. *No.* Says *no* much more often than *yes* in all endeavors.

3. **Self-sufficient.** Befits those who no longer ask for themselves, only for others.

4. **Self-scrutiny.** Exalts self-scrutiny and defends itself in justice, distant from hypocrisy.

5. **Difficulties.** Exhibits difficult understanding, less agreeable execution, and not-always-sympathetic performance without immediate results in everyday life.

6. **Qualification.** Supports itself through the active reactions of more mature individuals, independent of public opinion, prioritizing the quality of services rendered.

7. **Mentalsomatics.** Utilizes new ideas, discernment and the capacity of individuals to think freely, or rather, to have alert and active *mentalsomas*.

8. **Rationality.** Addresses itself to the essence of beings and factual contents through rationalized and non-repressive consciential preventative techniques.

9. **Awakening.** Has its persuasive nature based on discernment – essentially the awakening of *evolutionary sleepers* of all types, anywhere.

10. **Holo-maturity.** Dedicates itself to integral maturity of consciousness and *self-mastery of serenism* as goals. It is also selective about the means used to achieve its libertarian results.

11. **Existential series.** Is focused on intraphysical consciousness and explains the *whys* and *hows* of things in order for all consciousnesses to be liberated from the repetitive cycle of existential series.

12. **Truth.** While displaying leading-edge relative truth it demands nothing, talks of good nature and leisure while rejecting the conventions and temporalities of intraphysical society.

13. **Evolutionality.** Always insists on the many successive and unavoidable existential seriations to come, and on the reasons why we must accelerate our consciential evolution.

14. *Crutches.* Employs only those *psychological crutches* that are inevitable in human life – all the while explaining them, combating them and offering means for liberation from them.

15. **Liberation.** Applies the formulas of psychological liberation and self-responsibility.

BOTH THE CLARIFICATION TASK AND PENTA (PERSONAL ENERGETIC TASK) ARE PROCEDURES THAT ARE TO BE EXECUTED BY ADULTS.

16. **Uninhibitedness.** Seeks the consensus of universal discernment through a summation of ideas in public debates, making individuals uninhibited regarding real life.

17. **Maxi-universalism.** Supplies the motivated consciousness with the means for liberating him or herself from form, space and time, and finally arriving at maxi-universalism, without an *"ivory tower"*.

18. **Experiments.** Conveys the individual to think for his or herself, in order to tame the animal instincts through personal experiments, thus substituting belief with direct knowledge.

19. **Self-mastery.** Dispenses with personality cults, gurus, excessive dependence and systematic indoctrinations.

20. **Self-knowledge.** Operates independently of dispensable theological and intermediary temporal empires, in the enduring work of greater self-knowledge.

IN THE EVOLUTIONOLOGY OF CONSCIOUSNESS, THE CLARIFICATION TASK IS ALWAYS A MORE ADVANCED UNDERTAKING.

12. INSTRUMENTS FOR EXECUTING THE EXISTENTIAL PROGRAM

WE ARE CURRENTLY EXPERIENCING THE MOST INTENSELY ACCELERATED PERIOD OF HUMAN HISTORY THAN HAS EVER OCCURRED IN ANY OF OUR PREVIOUS LIVES.

Evolution. The last 2 centuries have been evolutionarily more illuminating for *terrestrial conscientiality* than all the millenniums of human life in this School-hospital.

Stimuli. Sociological studies made in the United States of America in 1995 calculate that the average person in western society, receives a *daily* average of 65,000 *more* units of stimulation than an identical individual in the past century.

Abundance. We live in an age that provides a greater abundance of the following 3 categories of *sustenance for intraphysical consciousness* than in any other period of intraphysical life on this planet:

1. **Holochakrality.** Sustenance through interconsciential energies: holo-chakrality, multiple deprivations and thosenology (study of thosenes).
2. **Somatics.** Sustenance of stomachs: hunger, soma and a more dignified healthy human existence and survival.
3. **Mentalsomatics.** Sustenance of the mentalsoma: acquisition of priority information for our discernment body.

Culture. We have never been so *knowledgeable* about so many multiform things. There are more scholarly individuals today than in any other century in human history.

Science. There are more scientists alive in the current phase of history than in the entire past of terrestrial beings. As *you know*, science is the *least imperfect* of all lines of human knowledge as it demands research and refutation with theories on leading-edge relative truth.

Child. Specialists have compared IQ tests in various countries (1996), and have shown that the average intelligence of a child nowadays, is comparable to that of a near-genius from only *5 decades* ago.

Information. A 10-year-old child currently *knows more*, or has already received more information relevant to his or her life, than the entire body of information possessed by Galileo Galilei, one of the pioneers of modern science, in his lifetime.

Age. Intraphysical life has never been so propitious for consciential evolution as it is now. Three centuries ago, cities were extremely fortified citadels, whose inhabitants – *ourselves* – lived in a state of continuous war with each other. For this and other reasons, individuals rarely lived to the age of 30 in the beginning of the XIX century.

Demographics. The terrestrial population has more than doubled (demographic explosion) from 1950, 2,500,000,000 persons, to 1996, 5,750,000,000 human inhabitants breathing on the planet.

Encounters. Today, you encounter a greater number of persons in only 1 week than you could have met during a 50-year lifetime in the Middle Ages, assuming you would have lived that long.

Mega-fraternity. As we know, encountering others is an indispensable resource in the exercising of mega-fraternity, within the structure of consciential evolution. No one evolves alone.

THE EARTH CURRENTLY PRESENTS THE BEST ENVIRONMENT FOR THE PRACTICE OF MEGA-FRATERNITY BY ALL CONSCIOUSNESSES.

Contemporaneity. This is why our current life, being one of *critically high quality in evolutionary terms*, has a value, for example, equivalent to 10 human lives, selected from the majority of those that we experienced in previous centuries.

Intelligence. Aside from the preceding exposition, no one, paradoxically, would affirm (and with good reason) that there exist, for example, 50 million intelligent, self-aware intraphysical consciousnesses who are developed beyond the unthinking masses (existential robotization), in the world in which we currently live. We are still not that far removed from the chimpanzee and gorilla.

Horror. The XX century is the greatest horror chamber that has existed in humanity (i.e., the First and Second World Wars, the Holocaust, regional armed conflicts). There have never existed so many people in need of cosmoethical conscientiality in this consciential dimension, awaiting the unified execution of our existential programs within the clarification task and polykarmality in solidarity.

Exclusions. Billions of consciousnesses (intraphysical and extraphysical) are awaiting our unified assistance. Just as *social exclusion* exists in intraphysical society, where there is a great number of individuals who are excluded from social benefits, or those with *no land, no roof, no employment, no salary* and even with *no personal computer*, there also exists *para-social exclusion*, in which we can include billions of *non-lucid* consciousnesses or para-psychotic post-mortems in the para-tropospheric extraphysical societies of this planet.

Thosenology. Let us nevertheless remain optimistic. It is especially relevant to consider that the thosene is the elementary instrument for the *manifestation of consciousness*.

STRICTLY SPEAKING, THE ELEMENTARY INSTRUMENT FOR THE EXECUTION OF ONE'S EXISTENTIAL PROGRAM *IS, LOGICALLY, THE ORTHOTHOSENE* (COSMOETHICAL THOSENE).

Resources. There are always various resources or auxiliary instruments that we can use in order to establish the goals of an existential program and correctly complete it. Among the many that exist, we can point out the following 11, listed here in order of natural personal development:

A. **Discipline.** Evolutionary self-organization.

B. **Self-evaluation.** Conscientiometry or conscientiometric measurements.
C. **Institution.** Conscientiocentrism or the conscientiocentric institution.
D. **VS.** Mastery of the vibrational state (VS), providing self-cure and self-defense.
E. **Recycling.** Intraconsciential and existential recycling (see glossary).
F. **Existential Inversion** (see glossary).
G. **Duo.** Constitution of an evolutionary duo (see glossary).
H. **Wholesaling.** Employment of a consciential wholesale approach.
I. **Conscientiality.** Execution of consciential gestations (see glossary).
J. **Penta.** Execution of the daily personal energetic task or penta.
K. **Self-relays.** Consciential self-relays (see glossary).

1. **Self-organization.** The best manner for an intraphysical consciousness to become anchored to the completion of the existential program is through self-organization.

EVOLUTIONARY SELF-ORGANIZATION IS BASED ON ALL DISCIPLINARY PROCESSES THAT ARE CAPABLE OF IMPOSING GOOD HABITS ON THE INDIVIDUAL.

Habits. Among an intraphysical consciousness' good habits it is always intelligent to include the creation and maintenance of a *intraphysical personal planner*.

Planner. There are 2 types of personal planner:
A. **Old.** In a book, with written daily annotations.
B. **Modern.** In a computer program (typed in a personal *notebook* or *laptop* computer), the ideal process for those who have the financial resources.

2. **Conscientiometry.** The measurements of consciousness, through the techniques, methods and tests offered by conscientiometry, allow the establishment of positive bases for the mathematization of intraphysical consciousness with respect to its evolutionary dynamic.

CONSCIENTIOMETRIC MEASUREMENTS IMMENSELY FAVOR THE EXECUTION OF THE EXISTENTIAL PROGRAM.

Tests. As well as the above-mentioned Conscientiogram, the book *"700 Conscientiology Experiments"* presents 300 priority conscientiometric tests for the motivated individual.

3. **Conscientiocentrism.** A conscientiocentric institution that concentrates its objectives on consciousness, per se, and on its evolution, can contribute greatly towards the creation and the dynamics of the personal existential program's execution, most notably in the case of the greater poly-karmic existential program.

Institutions. Following are 2 examples of conscientiocentric institutions:

A. **Institute.** The International Institute of Projectiology and Conscientiology (IIPC).
B. **Cooperative.** The IIPC Collaborators' Cooperative (CEAEC).

Examples. Functioning as consciential cooperatives in conscientiological society, based on employment and consciential ties, these institutions aim to serve as examples for conscientiological enterprises in this still pathological intraphysical society.

Bond. The consciential bond is that which is established between consciousnesses and enterprises in intraphysical society, in a self-aware, voluntary, poly-karmic and more evolved manner than the employment bond.

Groupality. The objective of the consciential bond is the practice of team spirit in the execution of clarification tasks and existential programs in group.

Dual. A dual simultaneous employment and consciential tie can intentionally occur with the same collaborator in a singular conscientiocentric enterprise.

4. **VS.** The VS or *vibrational state* is a technical condition for the maximal acceleration of the holochakra's (energetic parabody) consciential energies, through the impulse of the will.

Self-defense. The vibrational state can help maintain personal health and interconsciential self-defense within the intraphysical consciousness' holothosene, thus promoting the execution of his or her existential program.

Signs. One of the effects that the vibrational state predisposes is the identification of the individual's *energetic and parapsychic signs* (energetic, intraconsciential or animic and parapsychic signs), the self-aware employment of which can contribute greatly towards the execution of the individual existential program.

5. **Existential recycling.** Existential recycling is the technique for renovation of consciousness, without which it becomes impracticable to create the new undertakings that are adequate for better existential programs.

Intraconsciential recycling. A natural effect of existential recycling is intraconsciential recycling or the individual's, cosmoethical, inner reformation that begins with cerebral or neuronal renovation.

NEW SYNAPSES, OR NEURONAL CONNECTIONS, FACILITATE THE ADJUSTMENT OF THE EXISTENTIAL PROGRAM WITH THE ACQUISITION OF ORIGINAL IDEAS.

Group of existential recyclers. The existential recyclers' group promotes meetings and group exchanges, that objectify the execution of planned existential recycling.

Groupality. An existential recyclers' group can doubtless contribute towards the better execution of the individual existential program, whether it is group-karmic or poly-karmic in nature.

Revision. Periodic consciential self-evaluation does not generate any kind of demerit for the evaluator, but implies a reviewing of social postures and personal concepts.

Errors. Self-evaluation helps to reveal our errors and omissions in order that they may be corrected, inevitably resulting in our embarking on new paths through existential recycling.

6. **Existential inversion.** Existential inversion is the technique of rationally anticipating the evolutionary manifestations that are generally executed in the final period of intraphysical life by performing them in the initial period of adolescence or at a younger age.

Anticipation. These anticipated evolutionary acts or those that are developed prior to the biological maturity of the human body (soma), offer better results in the execution of our existential program.

Tool. Existential inversion is a tool or method that allows one to facilitate the completion of one's existential program. For the majority of young people, this should not be interpreted or understood as being the existential program, per se.

Invertor. The lucid existential invertor can be defined in the following manner: an intraphysical consciousness who initiates the execution of the existential program with self-awareness from early on.

Group of existential invertors. The existential invertors' group promotes meetings and group exchanges, that objectify the execution of planned existential inversions.

Youth. An existential invertors' group can greatly contribute towards the youths' successful execution of his or her individual existential programs, whether they be group-karmic or poly-karmic in nature.

7. **Duo.** An evolutionary duo is the condition in which 2 consciousnesses interact positively in *united evolution*.

THE EVOLUTIONARY DUO PERFORMS ITS EVOLUTIONARY WORK BASED ON THAT WHICH IS MOST PLEASURABLE IN HUMAN LIFE: RECIPROCAL LOVE.

Intercooperation. The evolutionary duo creates an existential condition of intercooperative evolution between two individuals. This condition provides the greatest aid for the simultaneous execution of both partners' existential program.
Joining. The joining of 2 lucid intraphysical consciousnesses inevitably also unites 2 pre-arranged existential programs.
Mutuality. In the condition of evolutionary duo, each partner has to simultaneously analyze his or her own existential program as well as the existential programs of both partners, in a reciprocal and incontestable manner, and in mutual cooperation.
Contention. One of the natural sources of contention in the holothosene of an evolutionary duo that demands judicious adjustments and more serious concessions on both parts, is when one of the intraphysical consciousnesses has a *macro-soma*.

Cases. In many cases, a macro-soma is provided in order for the individual to complete a greater existential program or existential maxi-program.
Conflict. If only one of the partners has a regular *soma* for the execution of a lesser existential program, this can generate a degree of conflict.
Seclusion. The *twofold loving seclusion* of an evolutionary duo, prepares 2 intraphysical consciousnesses for the ample practice of mega-fraternity starting *at home*, from within or from the 2 individuals themselves.
Clarification task. The love of an evolutionary duo only matures and becomes complete with the execution of the clarification task, poli-karmality and mega-fraternity, within the *groupal existential program* of 2 intraphysical consciousnesses.

Mega-fraternity. Mega-fraternity is absolute love, the condition of "post-graduate love", a *less-imperfect imperfection* in intraphysical life.

8. **Wholesaling.** Consciential wholesaling is the system of personal behavior based on the consolidation of healthy consciential acts.

Signatures. In the experience of consciential wholesaling, we utilize our personal thosenology without creating any negative, unhealthy or anti-cosmoethical traces or evolutionary rifts or *gaps*, as we leave *thosenic signatures* in our wake wherever we go.

CONSCIENTIAL WHOLESALING IS A PERSONAL PHILOSOPHY, INTRAPHYSICAL POLICY, OR THE IDEAL PRACTICE FOR THE EXECUTION OF AN EXISTENTIAL PROGRAM.

Retailing. *Consciential wholesaling* is superior to consciential retailing, an elementary system of individual behavior that is characterized by isolated, lesser consciential acts having minimal productive or evolutionary results.

Effects. Consciential retailing is not sufficient for the generation of constructive repercussions within maxi-fraternity, nor does it create notable evolutionary effects in vulgar intraphysical consciousnesses who have unsophisticated existential programs.

9. **Gestations.** Consciential gestations are the human consciousness' useful evolutionary end-products, within the personal framework of more advanced programming.

Groupal. The more common groupal consciential gestations are those that are developed by an evolutionary duo, through works performed with the consciential clarification task.

10. **Penta.** Penta *(p + en + ta)* is the daily, multidimensional energetic task, that involves the permanent assistance of the helpers and the technical transmission of consciential energies on the part of a human consciousness directly to extraphysical or projected consciousnesses.

Supports. The majority of intraphysical consciousnesses are still in the intraphysical *pre-penta* phase, seeking to improve the quality of the personal holothosene and set the 4 following fundamental pillars or supports of the existential program's edifice:

A. **Sentiment.** The support of sentiment or affective-sexual life, constituting an evolutionary duo.
B. **Professionality.** The support of professionality or of human survival without parasitism or dependency on other intraphysical consciousnesses.
C. **Intellectuality.** The support of lucid intellectuality or of the mentalsoma.
D. **Bioenergetics.** The support of high-quality personal, consciential energies, applied on a daily basis.

LET US BE COSMOETHICALLY EFFICIENT IN THE EXECUTION OF OUR EXISTENTIAL PROGRAM IN ORDER TO REPAY THE ASSISTANCE OF THE HELPERS.

Assistance. The personal energetic task (penta), that is performed in the normal waking state for the rest of the intraphysical life of the practitioner, tends to sustain the permanent extraphysical assistance and aid of the helpers.

Extraphysical clinic. The practice of penta allows the correct execution of the *intraphysical consciential epicenter consciousness' (key operational intraphysical consciousness) existential program* for the creation and maintenance of the extraphysical clinic.

11. Self-relay. Self-relay is the advanced condition in which a more lucid consciousness evolves by consecutively interweaving various intraphysical existences together.

Existential maxi-programs. Self-relay obviously offers extraordinary help towards the execution of existential maxi-programs through multiple somas, lives, societies and centuries.

Alternation. The ideal life is an alternating one, in which the intraphysical consciousness: is mainly concerned with, or occupies 75% of his or her consciential time with, intraphysical life, without discarding extra-somatic experiences; and occupies 25% of his or her consciential time with extraphysical life. This allows the individual to interlace the personal existential program with consciential self-relays, within the multi-existential cycle.

Interconnection. Through self-relay, or *existential continuism*, the evolving consciousness establishes a plan for the interweaving of his or her *interconnected existential programs*, together with the evolutionary orientor of the individual's karmic group.

Existential series. These interconnected existential programs act like links in a long chain (existential series), within one's *multi-existential cycle*.

DO YOU, AS A HUMAN BEING, FEEL MORE OR LESS ADAPTED TO THE ACTIVE EXECUTION OF YOUR EXISTENTIAL PROGRAM?

Helper. In rare instances, a helper will make a suggestion or inform the assisted intraphysical consciousness about some clause in the existential program, according to the directions of the evolutionary orientor.

13. MACRO-SOMATICS

Definition. The macro-soma *(macro + soma)* is a super-customized soma (human body). It is a resource that exists only for the execution of a specific extraphysical program that falls within 1 of 2 existing categories: an existential maxi-program or an existential mini-program.

Synonymy. These 2 expressions are synonymous with *macro-soma: super-tailor-made body; super-customized body.*

Macro-somatics. In macro-somatics, the science that studies the macro-soma, 2 fundamental types of macro-soma can be clearly distinguished, according to human gender:

A. **Woman.** The gyno-soma *(gyno + soma)* or feminine human body or that body which is specific to women.
B. **Man.** The andro-soma *(andro + soma)* or masculine body or that body which is specific to men.

THE GYNO-SOMA, ENSLAVED TO SEX AND ITS CONSEQUENCES, HAS SABOTAGED THE EXISTENTIAL MAXI-PROGRAMS OF LEGIONS OF WOMEN.

Prison. This can be translated as being the *double imprisonment* of consciousness to ego-karma and group-karma. It occurs much more frequently with women than with men, due to the greater sophistication of the feminine psychological, hormonal and sexual mechanisms.

Aphrodisiacal. We cannot forget that, in human sexuality, the gyno-soma is the aphrodisiacal body.

Menopause. Menopause causes legions of women to end up looking like dried up men towards the end of human life.

Eunuchs. Worst of all, many of these women uselessly carry a *dead gyno-chakra (sex-chakra)*; that is to say, they become men, so to speak and, furthermore, eunuchs.

Sex. The practicing of the vibrational state and daily sex, as well as the adequate use of hormones, can avoid this tragedy in the execution phase of life, shown as being the period between 36 and 70 years of age.

Execution. The execution phase of human life generally consolidates the realization of the existential program, possibly being the most productive phase of one's existential program, even for women.

Feminism. The feminist women's liberation movement, as well as female doctors, especially when *retired*, should concern themselves with menopause to a greater degree.

Solitary confinement. Is there a worse prison or solitary confinement than the period of menopause that, when complicated, affects, emaciates and prematurely kills millions of women in all countries, regardless of social class?

Vigor. In the period of fertile vigor, a woman can be freer than ever before, when she wishes to exalt, often erroneously, the power of her body over consciousness.

THE SOCIAL AND CIVIC POWER OF THE GYNO-SOMA OVER SOMATIC CONSCIOUSNESS IS A REACTION OF THE BELLY-BRAIN.

Prostitution. Unhappily, this social and political power of the gyno-soma has been better known, since antiquity, through the traditions of professional prostitution.

Half-dead. Finding herself in the menopausal period and without sexual vigor, a woman needs to be more discerning, alert and mature in order to confront her not uncommon condition of being energetically half-dead.

Mentalsoma. The menopausal period can be put to use in the emphasis of feminine consciousness over her soma, a reaction which, in this case, is generated by the mentalsoma. This allows one to take advantage of this phase of the gyno-soma's declining vitality.

Hormones. Chemical substances, including hormones and neurotransmitters, are extremely important in intraphysical life.

ENDORPHIN, A *NEUROTRANSMITTER*, IS A NATURALLY OCCURRING COCAINE *IN OUR BODY, THAT CAN EVEN DEVELOP A DEPENDENCY OR AD- DICTION.*

Marathons. Regarding endorphin, it is enough to see marathon fanatics, who are medical and psychological patients, addicted to running 4 miles every day. When they do not run, they become irritated and cranky.

14. EXISTENTIAL PROGRAM AND GEOGRAPHY

Geography. We can divide the areas of intraphysical consciousnesses' existential programs into 2 categories, relative to geography:

A. **Country dwelling intraphysical consciousnesses.** The country – a natural laboratory of the traditional – allows the rural farmer a greater introspection together with nature.
B. **City dwelling intraphysical consciousnesses.** The city – an artificial laboratory of the vanguard – permits, aside from all of its inconveniences, the technological city dwelling intraphysical consciousness a greater extroversion through the intensive communication and continued relationship with a greater number of individuals.

Laboratories. Both of these intraphysical laboratories facilitate the possibility for a consciousness to obtain a greater hyper-acuity and even become permanently-totally-intrusion-free, but the urban laboratory is always richer and more efficient for this purpose.

Modernity. The average urban citizen, at the end of the XX century, consumes several hundreds of times the energy that the farmer consumed a century ago, and enjoys a much higher standard of health, nutrition and comfort than any *king* of that era.

ALL THINGS ASIDE, ANY CITY IS MORE OF A SELF-EVOLUTIONARY BATTLE FRONT THAN THE COUNTRY.

Urbanite. An intraphysical consciousness in the city (urbanite), on account of encountering a greater number of persons daily, enjoys opportunities for more ample consciential gestations.

Home. Domestic life – at home, in a house or apartment – predisposes introspection, reflection and intraconsciential self-evaluation on the part of the lucid intraphysical consciousness. It is notably important in the performance of the existential program in the mega-city or on the evolutionary front line.

Agrarians. Even human gestations are simpler in the country, where children are raised by *mother nature*, sometimes much like livestock, in a spontaneous, instinctive manner.

ACCORDING TO THE PRINCIPLES OF MODERN ECOLOGY, THE COUNTRY IS NOT, MUST NOT AND CANNOT BE THE BACK YARD OF THE MEGA-CITY.

Nature. There are many ponderous myths and taboos about nature, rural life and indigenous people, but rural exodus is a daily phenomenon.

Arena. Nevertheless, evolutionary reality shows that the much criticized conglomeration of humans in the megalopolis or mega-city is still the best arena for the acceleration of consciential evolution.

Anti-city. The more intelligent option is to live in a city or mega-city, as long as it is not an *anti-city*, lacking security and quality of life that is adequate for the satisfactory execution of our existential program.

Obsolescence. The following 15 intraphysical habits have become or are becoming obsolete in our current city lives:

1. **Alcohol.** Discussing wines with total solemnity.
2. **Armor.** Wearing armor to defend oneself.
3. **Authors.** Reading Marx, Nordau and other outdated authors.
4. **Carriage.** Riding a horse-drawn carriage.
5. **Cart.** Using hand-arts.
6. **Enigmas.** Writing enigmatic letters.
7. **Spittoon.** Spitting in cuspidors or spittoons.

8. *Little world.* Using a dialect belonging to your own *little world.*
   9. **Kiosk.** Frequenting grandiose kiosks.
   10. **Serenades.** Performing romantic serenades.
   11. **Sonnets.** Writing sonnets.
   12. **Smoking.** Defending cigarettes, cigars or nicotine.
   13. **Pork skins.** Eating pork skins (cholesterol).
   14. **Plays on words.** Creating plays on words.
   15. **Urban development.** Building narrow streets in the city.

NEOPHILIA, WHEN BASED ON CONSCIENTIAL DISCERNMENT, ONLY AIDS THE EVOLUTION OF CONSCIOUSNESS.

15. EXISTENTIAL PROGRAM EXECUTION TECHNIQUE

Undertaking. All libertarian undertakings in the existential program and the clarification task exhibit 4 indispensable stages, in the following chronological order:

1. **Project.** The project is generally the easiest and quickest phase to be accomplished.
2. **Attempt.** The attempting of a preliminary execution and its first steps.
3. **Realization.** The actual realization of the project.
4. **Maintenance.** Maintenance – the most difficult and longest phase of the undertaking.

Beginning. To begin an undertaking is only to put it in gear, to take the first step, or make a superficial sketch.

Roots. The maintenance of an undertaking is the most complex task because it sends down roots in intraphysical-extraphysical life, creating a holothosene in the passage of time.

Constancy. Constancy or persistence in the work of an existential program provides an aura of calm and benevolence. Inflexibility, stubbornness, intransigence and radicalism *are not* the same as constancy.

Tasks. In the voluntary and satisfactory execution of the existential program, a consciousness has to clearly define the goals and personal tasks in the various stages of the experiment, from the cradle to the grave.

IN THE EXECUTION OF OUR EXISTENTIAL PROGRAM, WE HAVE TO CONSIDER THE LIFE PROJECT AND THE DEVELOPMENT OF A NATURAL TIMELINE.

Phases. In terms of an existential program's execution, human life can be divided into 2 technical phases:

A. **Preparation.** First, the *preparatory* phase, that spans from rebirth until 35 years of physical age.
B. **Execution.** Second, the *execution* phase from 36 to an average of 70 years of physical age.

Basement. In the preparatory phase, an intraphysical consciousness passes through the *consciential basement* (see glossary) and confronts formal education in the new terrestrial existence.

Profession. Still in the preparatory phase, the intraphysical consciousness prepares for a professional career, which is indispensable for financial self-sustenance devoid of parasitism of other persons, doctrines, businesses or the state.

Discernment. Only discernment permits the establishment of an exact delineation between personal, natural and hoped for ambition, and the adequate execution of the directives of the individual's existential program, notably for those who have reached 35 years of age.

Trinomial. In the execution phase, the intraphysical consciousness should already have defined his or her destiny for the rest of the current life, doing what he or she likes, within the *trinomial motivation-work-leisure*, and developing the existential program that they came to complete. We all came to human life to evolve, albeit with good humor, and happiness for whatever we do.

THE BROAD EXECUTION PHASE OF THE EXISTENTIAL PROGRAM PRECEDES THE DEACTIVATION OF THE HUMAN BODY, FOR THE MAJORITY OF INDIVIDUALS.

Prescriptions. Following are 5 technical prescriptions for success in the execution of one's existential program:

A. **Discipline.** Maintain personal discipline in daily conduct.
B. **Activity.** Avoid inactivity or a sedentary life.
C. **Conscientiality.** Seek the greatest mastery possible of consciousness over the soma.
D. **Will.** Trust in your strong will, that is capable of permitting magnanimous decisions without doubts or vacillations.
E. **Friendships.** Eliminate *idle friendships* with *evolutionary tourists*, those who only wish to have fun and ignore the principles of consciential evolution.

Evolution. Every existential program is established on the following 3 bases. It is important that the interested individual identify which of these characterizes the existential program:

A. **File.** Acceleration of your own ego-karmic evolution or the improvement of your *individual file*.
B. **Group-karma.** Evolution of your group-karma.
C. **Mini-piece.** Performance of poly-karmic works, with the intraphysical consciousness operating at a more advanced evolutionary level as a mini-piece (small cog) within an assistential maxi-mechanism.

WHAT ACTUALLY PROPELS YOUR LIFE PROGRAM: EGO-KARMALITY, GROUP-KARMALITY OR POLY-KARMALITY?

Error. The best formula or the simplest and most practical ideal in the execution of one's existential program is for an intraphysical consciousness not to allow errors to occur.

Mini-failures. Nevertheless, many existential completists have learned from their own errors: 2 or 3 small failures can more profoundly stimulate and challenge the individual to achieve existential completism.

Mother-thosene. In thosenology, the mother-thosene is the main idea or the master pillar; the thosenic synthesis or predominant thosene in a holothosene.

Self-scrutiny. Rationally speaking, if an intraphysical consciousness does not diagnose his or her own mother-thosene – that predominates in the personal holothosene – with a maximum of self-scrutiny in the current evolutionary period of intraphysicality, it will become more difficult for the individual to characterize the directives of his or her existential program and the bases of existential recycling.

Strong traits. Among individual patterns of conduct, postures or ideal *strong* traits needed for the pre-serenissimus intraphysical consciousness (ordinary individual) to optimize efforts, potentialize performance and execute existential program fairly well, taking maximum advantage of the evolutionary possibilities of 1 intraphysical life, we can point out the following 5 facets:

1. Form an evolutionary duo.
2. Sponsor consciential gestations.
3. Practice penta.
4. Achieve the condition of consciential epicenter.
5. Promote periodic personal existential recycling in order to correct the path of your existential program's chronological development.

EACH EVOLUTIONARY SUCCESS DEMANDS A CERTAIN DEGREE OF EFFORT, PERSEVERANCE AND INDIVIDUAL PERFORMANCE.

16. THE "IS STILL NOT" TECHNIQUE

IT IS POINTLESS TO OPPOSE LEADING-EDGE RELATIVE REALITY: SELF-CORRUPTION DOES NOT PROMOTE OUR INTERCONSCIENTIAL IMPROVEMENT.

Still. The *"is still not"* technique aptly expresses the evolutionary priorities for all those interested in making intelligent choices regarding the development of the existential program, the clarification task, poly-karmality and the positive balance of his or her personal holo-karmic account.

Conditions. Following are 13 examples of the *"still not it"* technique:

1. **Self-relay.** The greatest tropospheric intraphysical consciousness *is still not* a self-relaying intraphysical consciousness.
2. **Wholesaling.** The greatest retailing *is still not* consciential wholesaling.
3. **Self-awareness.** The greatest lucid projection *is still not* multi-dimensional self-awareness.
4. **Science.** The greatest art *is still not* science, in terms of evolutionary realities.
5. **Permanently-totally-intrusion-free.** The greatest, most successful exorcism *is still not* the condition of being conscientially permanently-totally-intrusion-free.
6. **Discernment.** Foremost good sense *is still not* technical discernment.
7. **Duo.** The greatest passion between two individuals *is still not* a well constituted evolutionary duo.
8. **Fact.** The greatest theory *is still not* proven fact.
9. **Hyper-acuity.** The greatest of "Nobel Prize winning qualities" *is still not* hyper-acuity.

10. **Holomaturity.** The greatest empiricism *is still not* holomaturity.

11. **Realization.** The greatest discourse *is still not* sound realization.

12. **Clarification task.** The greatest consolation task *is still not* the clarification task.

13. **Penta.** The greatest parapsychic passivity *is still not* penta.

Congruence. What is important is the authenticity of our evolutionary congruence in these 3 binomials: theorice (theory & practice), verbaction (verbalization & action) and coform (content & form).

SELF-CORRUPTION IS TO STEAL FROM OURSELVES: RICHNESS, LIBERTY, TIME, HEALTH, SPACE, OPPORTUNITIES AND CONSCIENTIAL ENERGIES.

17. EXISTENTIAL ANTI-PROGRAM

Definition. The *existential anti-program* is a personal condition of the intraphysical consciousness that manifests through one's acts, attitudes and postures against the rational execution of his or her existential programming.
Synonymy. Equivalent expression for *existential anti-program*: *existential self-disorganization*.

THERE ARE INTRAPHYSICAL CONSCIOUSNESSES, WHO ARE VICTIMS OF EXISTENTIAL ROBOTIZATION, WHO HAVE NEVER THOUGHT ABOUT THE EXISTENTIAL PROGRAM.

Theory. Other *seated-on-the-fence* intraphysical consciousnesses intellectually discover the existence of the personal existential program and go no further than that.
Practice. Other more lucid and organized intraphysical consciousnesses live their lives with the execution of their clearly-identified existential program in view.
Experience. The evolutionary results of the human experience of each of these intraphysical consciousnesses are extremely diverse, independent of the modalities of their para-genetics, genetics, social-cultural-environmental influence, formal education or the bases of their existential programs.
Social-cultural-environmental influence. Social-cultural-environmental influence is one of the most potent holothosenes in intraphysical life, capable of annulling talents and the existential programs of legions of intraphysical consciousnesses.
Concessions. The majority of individuals who know their evolutionary path but are not able to realize it in a satisfactory manner suffer some kind of intrusive influence from their acquaintances (intraphysical and extraphysical consciousnesses).

Interprison. These intrusive influences are frequently due to unresolved issues in the intraphysical consciousness' recent past, in a condition of group-karmic interprison.

Postures. Following is a list of 18 existential anti-program postures, among innumerous others:

A. Para-genetics.
B. Intrudability (victimization).
C. Lack of personal discernment.
D. Hypomnesic syndrome.
E. Personal de-education.
F. Cultural *status*.
G. Intraphysical melancholy.
H. Consciential regression to infancy.
I. Personal neophobia.
J. Shock from neothosenes.
K. *Seated-on-the-fence condition.*
L. Perfectionism.
M. Indecisiveness.
N. Ignorance.
O. Belly-brain adoration.
P. Promiscuity.
Q. Abortions.
R. Cryogenics.

1. **Para-genetics.** Those consciousnesses with a relatively greater inner balance always bring with them, through innate ideas (para-genetics), the final proposal or the magnanimous objectives of his or her existential program.

MANY INDIVIDUALS AVOID ACCEPTING THE PRESSURE OF THEIR INNATE IDEAS AND THUS ALIENATE THEMSELVES, DUE TO FRANK SELF-CORRUPTION.

2. **Intrudability.** Both ostensive and disguised intrudability (self-intrusion, first; hetero-intrusion, second), impede the

ability of the intraphysical consciousness to recycle his or her undertakings. Recycling would liberate them from repressions and inhibitions, thus allowing them to make concessions regarding, most notably, the following 5 conditions:

A. **Money.** Monetary wealth (liquid assets).
B. **Patrimony.** Assets or belongings (economics).
C. **Information.** Cutting-edge privileged information.
D. **Sociability.** Prestige or social *status*.
E. **Power.** Temporal power.

Millionaires. Extraphysical intruders are the greatest specialists in fomenting the creation of belly-brained millionaires in all countries, thus annulling, not rarely, individual and groupal existential programs.

EXTRAPHYSICAL INTRUDERS GENERALLY IGNORE THE DETAILS OF OUR EXISTENTIAL PROGRAM.

Evidence. Only with the passage of time and the execution of the intraphysical consciousness' existential program, will the evidence of leading-edge relative truths arise and the intruders be able to identify the details of the individual's existential program.

Existential maxi-program. Intruders are more easily able to identify works intended by intraphysical consciousnesses in cases of existential maxi-programs that clearly involve the defense of the clarification task and poly-karmality.

Small groups. Given this context, the intruders arm themselves and, not rarely, even form small groups of extraphysical consciousnesses who are *satellites of intruders*, used in order to maintain the dominions of heavy interconsciential vampirizations, at any cost.

Front. In some holothosenes, the intruders form a type of *broad front of intrusion* against the clarification of their ignorant, vulnerable, human or tropospheric energetic victims.

Mishaps. As you can see, intrusion-based parapsychic mishaps can compromise the execution of an existential program when they reach a high level of intensity or frequency, thus impeding the manifestations of intraphysical consciousness.

3. *Anti*-discernment. Thosenity, when derived directly from the belly-brain, is generally characterized by irrationality, anti-discernment and low self-esteem, which ends up generating existential *anti*-program attitudes.

Victimization. Only the *half-baked intraphysical consciousness*, in terms of evolution, becomes a victim of anti-discernment, or rather: of him or herself.

Self-complacency. Within the directives of the cosmoethic, when they are well understood, one must avoid *hetero*-complacency, signifying impunity, and *self*-complacency, signifying negligence, laziness or carelessness, which lead to existential incompletism.

Results. Evolution and consciential intraphysical performance are not based on evaluation of the individual's existential program per se, but rather, on the evaluation of the results of the individual's existential program.

4. **Syndrome.** The *hypomnesia syndrome*, wherein an intraphysical consciousness partially forgets the directives of his or her path and its tasks in human life, can be psychologically generated as a form of alienation from intraphysical duties in the execution of the existential program.

IN THE HYPOMNESIA SYNDROME, THE ATTITUDE OF ALIENATION CHARACTERIZES A TYPE OF INSTINCTIVE OR UNCONSCIOUS SELF-CORRUPTION.

5. **De-education.** Even formal education, that helps to improve so many of us, can be ambiguous and become transformed into a process of alienation for the intraphysical consciousness (de-education) from the execution and completion of the existential program.

6. *Status.* Many people obtain a university diploma and coast to the side of the road, away from the evolutionary path, under the effect of their new cultural, professional or economic *status* facilitated by graduation.

7. **Intraphysical melancholy.** One's deep emotional bruises are eradicated or reduced with the elimination of intraphysical melancholy.

Prevention. The *prevention of intraphysical melancholy* can be effected through the researching of one's own existential program, self-motivation and the execution of clarification tasks that have been neglected, within a personal search through the lasting practice of mega-fraternity.

8. **Regression.** When an individual exalts his or her childhood as being the best period of this life, lamenting over adult life, it is because they are escaping from the unfinished, frustration and, worst of all, through a mechanism of ego regression.

INFANCY IS A PREPARATORY PHASE. THE CHILD IS A HUMAN CONSCIOUSNESS THAT IS STILL RESTRICTED TO A GREAT DEGREE.

Universalism. There are those who, having the intention of practicing mega-fraternity, universalism, holism, transdisciplinarity and even polyglotism, bring together diverse but apparently similar techniques from different lines of thought that are, nevertheless, often essentially contradictory.

Holothosene. This mentalsomatic and unifying work demands effort on the part of the neophilic intraphysical consciousness, in order to harmoniously bring together, compose, wed or amalgamate the different principles within the universe of leading-edge relative truths or of a singular groupal holothosene.

Neophilia. Neophilia is the easy adaptation of an intraphysical consciousness to new situations, ambiences, things and occurrences.

Coherence. In conscientiology, neophilia is the personal predisposition towards evolutionary renovation, an obligation of the intraphysical consciousness to him or herself, in order to remain coherent and free of self-corruptions.

Motivation. Upon seeking to reposition him or herself and assume new obligations stimulated by his or her neophilia, the intraphysical consciousness prepares him or herself with great aptitude and motivation for the reasonable execution of the existential program.

MOTIVATION IS A HEALTHY LONGING FOR THE NEW *(NEOPHILIA)* THAT ACCELERATES THE EVOLUTIONARY WORK OF THE EXISTENTIAL PROGRAM.

Simplism. The complexity of the consciential micro-universe (one's individual world) explains why simple-minded neophobic intraphysical consciousnesses cannot tolerate a more advanced level of leading-edge relative truths in any sector of consciousness research.

9. **Neophobia.** Neophobia is the fear of new or original things, the opposite of neophilia.

10. **Shock.** For the neophobic intraphysical consciousness, the sophisticated harmonization of evolved concepts constitutes a *shock of holothosenes* that often promotes an intraconsciential imbalance and a greater personal insecurity.

Schism. This shock of holothosenes can finally generate a dissidence of ideas, creating a schism (gap) in the intraphysical consciousness relative to his or her karmic group.

Utopia. A dissidence or schism, in this case, can generate a utopia (alienation) in regards to the execution of the existential program (clarification task, poly-karmality) in group.

11. **Jettison.** It is important, however, to rationally emphasize one fact regarding existential anti-program manifestations in this context: what is not evolutionarily useful, is truly not useful and should be disregarded and jettisoned.

Seated-on-the-fence. It is of no use to try to camouflage or sugar-coat things, or childishly desire to please everyone.

Universalism. Universalism is not the same as being *seated-on-the-fence.*

12. **Perfectionism.** Absolute perfection does not exist in intraphysical life. The obvious consensus in terms of conscious evolution is that it is best to do things well.

Banalities. Nevertheless, it is never ideal to waste time, energy and opportunities with perfectionist banalities.

News. There are at least 2 categories of perfectionism: theoretical and practical. In the end, both are dispensable and generally noxious.

Theory. Theoretical perfectionism is the worst and is frequently based on philosophical principles or elaborations.

PERFECTIONISM OBSTRUCTS THE FULL APPLICATION OF THEORICE (THEORY + PRACTICE) AND TRAMPLES THE DYNAMISM OF THE EXISTENTIAL PROGRAM'S EXECUTION.

Parapsychologists. One of parapsychology's basic omissions is that parapsychologists ignore the details of their existential program. The majority seem not to be at all concerned with this issue.

Self-mimicry. The majority of parapsychologists unnecessarily repeat (self-mimicry) *ad nauseam* what previous researchers – their and pioneers idols from the past – did in their fields of research.

Inactivity. Many parapsychologists, upon losing the dynamism of their current human life through lack of renovation, handicap the realization of their respective existential programs due to these dispensable self-mimicries.

Theorice. Other parapsychologists do not embrace theorice, the employment of their consciential energies and parapsychism, remaining mere theoreticians in the role of non-participatory researchers, thus jeopardizing their existential programs.

Extraphysical consciousnesses. I am registering here this *modality of existential anti-program* in the area of parapathological perfectionism in order to respond to requests made by extraphysical consciousnesses that I have encountered while projected, who were parapsychic researchers in England.

Pioneers. These pioneers illustrate 2 ectopic behaviors – self-mimicry and non-participation – as being less intelligent in terms of consciential evolution.

Holomaturity. Generally, an intraphysical consciousness only acquires confidence in his or her progress towards a consciential objective, principles with integrity and maintains personal coherence (verbaction) when he or she attains a higher level of holomaturity

HOLOMATURITY IS EXPRESSED THROUGH THE SATISFACTORY RECUPERATION OF CONS, THE UNITS OF MEASUREMENT OF PERSONAL LUCIDITY.

13. **Indecision.** Our predisposition for vacillations, indecision, progress and regress become more obvious when the facts are analyzed over a longer period of time.

Facts. The following are 4 concrete facts as examples of our incoherence and vacillation:

A. **Field.** First, a man works hard in the field in order to have the means to live in the mega-city. Later, he works hard in order to leave the mega-city and return to country life or his native land.

B. **Gold.** First, a man works tirelessly in the mines to uncover the gold that is under the soil. Later, he works tirelessly to bury the gold that he uncovered in underground safe deposit boxes in banks, where it remains without direct contact, as it was before when under the ground.

C. **Fame.** First, a woman of 30 does everything she can to be famous and recognized wherever she goes. After she is 60, she does everything she can in order to not be recognized, using dark glasses and disguises wherever she goes, thereby avoiding the public she once conquered.

D. **Age.** First, a woman does everything she can to hide her shame of being 40 years old. Half-a-century later, she does whatever she can to boast and tell everyone that she is 90 years old.

Avoidance. It is intelligent to avoid progress and regress, vacillation and incoherence in our intraphysical life, seeking to execute our existential program in a straightforward manner, slowly and consistently, in order to achieve existential completion.

14. **Ignorance.** Human immaturities could fill an encyclopedia. Examples of spontaneous and natural ignorance abound. Some are not categorized as illnesses, but are part of the evolution of the consciential principle, including the following 3:

A. **Bats.** Bats think that night is day.
B. **Dogs.** Dogs chase cars.
C. **Man.** Primitive man has beliefs and is idolatrous.

DANGEROUS OR RADICAL SPORTS ARE OBVIOUSLY NOT INCLUDED IN THE EVOLUTIONARY PLANS OF AN EXISTENTIAL PROGRAM.

Abuse. Many people on the Earth still live without any existential plan and abuse their bodies, slumbering under the command of their *belly-brain*, just like our subhuman evolutionary colleagues: the lion, hyena or wolf, for example.

Resentment. Hatred, resentment, lamentations and hypersensitivity – the great inhibitors of team spirit, belonging to subhuman animals – are always elementary, primitive and atavistic manifestations of emotion.

Para-pathologies. Strictly speaking, resentments are derived from the para-pathologies of the psychosoma, with holo-chakral and somatic reflexes that are totally existential anti-program in nature.

Inexperience. The intraphysical society in which we live still acts with a reasonable degree of pathology due to our ignorance or evolutionary inexperience, and we are its component parts. This fact reaches all sectors of human life, even the area of Economics.

Success. Not everyone who has achieved personal, human success has an advanced existential program. There are legions of millionaires who are victims of lamentable ambivalence, and simultaneously suffer from and practice intraphysical intrusion.

Drugs. It is sad and regrettable to note that thousands of intraphysical consciousnesses who are addicted to drugs know that they are committing a slow suicide and, nevertheless, use escapism as a self-corrupt justification of preferring a short human life to the tedium of old age, the suffering of cancer or the problems arising from a stroke. These individuals have no notion of the existential program.

Happiness. An intraphysical consciousness who has done a good job of completing his or her existential mandate feels happier the longer they live. Old age, for example, can be the most joyful period of a man or woman's earthly existence.

15. **Adoration.** The adoration, deification or guru worship that many intraphysical consciousnesses engage in constitutes an error of evading personal responsibility concerning their own evolution.

Self-evaluation. By adoring a being who is considered to have greater qualities and potentialities, the individual presumes that he or she is exempt from performing self-evaluation and is free from their obligations, passing personal responsibilities to another.

ADORATION IS AN INFANTILE REACTION, CHARACTERISTIC OF THE CONSCIENTIAL BASEMENT. IT GENERATES DEVIATIONS FROM PERSONAL EXISTENTIAL PROGRAMS.

16. **Promiscuity.** Many promiscuous sexual relationships occur with the unsuspected participation of extraphysical consciousnesses who are ill or are in lack of consciential energies.

Re-somas. It is in this way that spurious and inopportune intraphysical re-somas or rebirths occur, having exclusively intrusive causes or due only to interconsciential intrusions.

Affairs. The practice of having *"one night stands"* and *brief affairs devoid of obligation,* characteristic of contemporary youth, as a function of the sexual promiscuity that it represents, can result in a condition of existential anti-program.

17. **Abortion.** These cases need to be analyzed as rationally as possible when addressing the issue of intentional abortions.

18. **Cryogenics.** A group of wealthy and optimistic individuals not resigned to de-soma (biological death) and who were, to a point, robotized by technology, decided to bet on the future, paying 120 thousand dollars each and offering up their lifeless bodies to cryogenics.

Freezer. The cadavers of these intraphysical consciousnesses are frozen and conserved in a type of *freezer* or sarcophagus, composed of an aluminum capsule inside of a steel cylinder.

Foundations. In the United States of America, there are 4 foundations dedicated to the cryogenic process, the technique of cooling used for maintaining bodies frozen, in this case the deactivated somas of the intraphysical consciousnesses buried in aluminum capsules.

Members. Extraphysical facts show that the intraphysical consciousnesses who are members of these foundations in charge of cryogenic processes have not experienced consciential openness in their existences through the occurrence of impactful lucid projections.

Embarrassment. This being the case, these consciousnesses, upon returning to the status of extraphysical consciousnesses through the consciential shock of de-soma, will obviously suffer manifest embarrassment with the reality they will find with respect to their extraphysical survival.

Extraphysical melancholy. Some of these extraphysical consciousnesses, when more lucid and with greater self-scrutiny, will obviously go through an *extraphysical melancholy*, upon recognizing their condition of *consciential ectopia* in regards to their existential program.

CRYOGENICS, WITH ALL OF ITS TECHNOLOGICAL APPARATUS, IS THE ULTIMATE ACT OF IGNORANCE IN TERMS OF CONSCIENTIAL MULTI-DIMENSIONALITY.

Apotheosis. Cryogenics is the frustrating and embarrassing apotheosis of an incomplete existential program (existential incompletion), crowned by a illusory bouquet of artificial flowers.

18. EXISTENTIAL PROGRAM AND CONSCIENTIAL ECTOPIA

Definition. *Consciential ectopia* is the unsatisfactory execution of an existential program – one being performed in an eccentric, dislocated manner far removed from the life project that was previously chosen during one's intermissive period to facilitate development of the human consciousness' intraphysical life.

Synonymy. These 2 expressions are equivalent to *consciential ectopia: alienation from existential program; dislocation from existential program.*

Adjustment. If one had prepared appropriately, they will now perform a role in a social condition that fits his or her temperament and aptitudes, within a well adjusted social atmosphere or holothosene.

Dislocation. If this does not occur, they will feel dislocated, performing an *ectopic existential program* that is off the mark, removed from the locale or in different conditions than those that were indicated, planned and, in many cases, chosen by the individual him or herself.

Anomaly. Ectopia presents itself in many forms, being an anomalous situation or distant from the conditions that an intraphysical consciousness had hoped for. The existential program is supposed to serve as a *nest* that should have been built by the individual for his or her shelter, but instead was neglected.

LEGIONS OF INTRAPHYSICAL CONSCIOUSNESSES LIVE UNDER THE COMMAND OF THE CEREBELLUM – AN ECTOPIA – AND NOT THE CEREBRUM; A PRIZE FIGHTER, FOR EXAMPLE.

Conditions. On the subject of ectopia, each human personality finds him or herself in 1 of 2 conditions regarding the programming of human life:

Existential Program Manual

A. **Adjustment.** Relatively happy with an adequate or correct existential program.
B. **Inadequate.** Permanently frustrated with an inadequate, dislocated or ectopic existential program.

Causes. Many factors of terrestrial life serve as causes for the functional dislocation of an existential program; including the following 10:

    A. **Sociability.** An agitated social life.
    B. **Company.** Bad company.
    C. **Exoticism.** Strange doctrines.
    D. **Routines.** Stagnating routines.
    E. **Stagnation.** Personal accommodations.
    F. **Retailing.** Consciential retailing.
    G. **Accidents.** Accidents due to negligence.
    H. **Neophobia.** Neophobia or fear of the new.
    I. **Intrusion.** Sabotage triggered by extraphysical intruders.
    J. **Factionalism.** Factionalism of the person's or group's own *little world*.

Ectopia. Practice of the consolation task can be an intraphysical ectopia in terms of the execution of an advanced existential program that involves the clarification task.

Recycling. Existential recycling is the only resource available for intelligently aborting a dislocated existential program, in the sense of an intraphysical consciousness being able to start afresh when already in the execution or applied phase of life.

Belief. Deep within him or herself, an intraphysical consciousness, upon confessing faith or belief, admits that the idol of adoration, that greater being or consciousness, will take care of them and will thus exempt them from obligations, installing a consciential ectopia in the existential program.

Procreation. There are women who are induced, beyond the instinctive forces of genetics or procreation, to have a child, without this having been included extraphysically in the intermissive course or existential program.

HOMOSEXUALITY AND LESBIANISM CAN BE CONSIDERED SEXO-SOMATIC ECTOPIA IN TERMS OF THE HUMAN SPECIES.

Causes. According to preceding observations, consciential ectopia can be caused by, among other things, adoration, the consolation task and cryogenics; generating, in this way, the dislocated existential program and extraphysical melancholy.

Alienation. Following are 12 types of ectopic consciential gestations, or alienating tasks, for rational analysis and logical avoidance in the performance of an existential program:

1. **Self-mimicry.** Personal complacency with repetitive and dispensable self-mimicry instead of executing the new tasks of one's *correct existential program*, that is healthy and was previously planned.
2. **Group-karma.** The incurable subjection – interprison – to the intraphysical consciousnesses of one's own karmic group without completing the poly-karmic tasks that had been planned.
3. **Intraphysicality.** Excessive personal (social) commitments with intraphysical existence – somatics – to the detriment of a program of multidimensional tasks.
4. **Mediumism.** Submission to the routines of an animic-mediumistic group instead of the accomplishment of the personal, isolated tasks of penta (daily personal energetic task).
5. **Mysticism.** The development of a personal existential program based on a mystical doctrine that is foreign to one's pre-established program in the area of research, logical refutation and leading-edge relative truths of conventional newtonian-cartesian science.
6. **Morality.** Permanence within the universe of human morality, without cosmoethical thosenes, which triggers existential programs that are faint and morally decadent.

7. **Basement.** Remaining stationary in the condition of the consciential basement instead of completing tasks that were programmed in one's most recent intermissive course.

8. **Projectability.** The experience only of spontaneous conscious projections, instead of conscious projections induced by the projector's iron clad will.

9. **Existential recycling.** The tardy realization of existential recycling – an imposition – instead of the program preestablished by choice, in the correct period and time, through existential inversion. The dislocated existential program should be intelligently aborted (existential recycling), in the same manner as a tubal pregnancy.

10. **Sectarianism.** The erroneous focusing of personal efforts within the limitations of sectarianism (factionalism, *one's own little world*), instead of practicing the maximum universalism possible.

11. **Consolation task.** Attachment to the ease of the consolation task instead of the more difficult and less agreeable development of the clarification task, due to the fact that the consolation task is an ectopia with regards to the advanced existential program.

12. **Retailing.** Departure towards the embankment of the retailing approach in one's conduct, instead of permanence on the path of the more evolved, self-aware, *consciential wholesaling*.

ONE OF THE WORST ECTOPIC HUMAN PRISONS THAT MUTILATES EXISTENTIAL PROGRAMS IS A BELIEF SYSTEM.

19. IDEOLOGICAL DISSIDENCE

Dissidence. Dissidence is the act of dissenting, like a group of corporate members who separate from a corporation due to a difference of opinion.

Synonymy. These 3 expressions are equivalent to dissidence: *secession; schism; dissension.*

Conscientiology. In conscientiology, dissidence is an inevitable consequence of the theorice (theory + practice) and verbaction (verbalization + action) of leading-edge relative truths or the practice of assistential clarification tasks.

Growth. In the performance and completion of an existential program, and notably in an existential maxi-program, leading-edge relative truths never bring one harmony and peace, but rather, healthy stress and growing crises for many people.

Group-karma. Growing crises inevitably generate ideological dissidents as a side-effect, beyond the performance, intervention or even the efforts and assistential dedication of the karmic group's personalities.

Dissident. The dissident, strictly speaking, is not our enemy, but an intraphysical consciousness who democratically disagrees with our ideas and statements; a natural positioning that we must respect.

THE DISSIDENT IS OUR ATYPICAL COLLABORATOR. THE ONE WHO SECEDES IN ORDER TO ALLOW US PASSAGE HELPS OUR WORK.

Cosmoethic. It is important, however, to point out that the problem that triggers the most dissidence, within the group work of conscientiology, is the least recognized by the dissidents themselves: the cosmoethic.

Friendship. Cosmoethically, ideological dissidence should not and can not affect the true friendship.

Ideologies. Friendship has to rise above ideological agreements and disagreements.

Education. The evolutionary education of consciousness puts leading-edge relative truths, little by little, above individuals.

Deficient. We know that legions of intraphysical consciousnesses, *consciential deficients* – including many categories of ideological dissidents – use limiting mechanisms that are social-cultural-environmental inheritances during his or her entire life, without arriving at a reasonable de-repression.

CONSCIENTIAL DEFICIENTS CRYSTALLIZE THEIR LIFE IN SACRALIZATION, STAYING IN THEIR OWN LITTLE WORLD AND IN EXISTENTIAL ROBOTIZATION.

Respect. Above all, however, the cosmoethic suggests that we respect the evolutionary level of all beings, without forcing them to accept one or another of our points of view, whether it is correct or wrong, evolved or anachronistic.

Thosenity. This posture characterizes the exact union between affectivity and discernment within the micro-universe of the intraphysical consciousness, or rather, the greater balance between the *tho* and *sen* of our lucid thosenity in interconsciential dealings.

Conflicts. With the comprehension of this cosmoethic conduct, the intraphysical consciousness no longer suffers 3 types of conflicts:

1. **Discrimination.** Discriminating against others.
2. **Susceptibilities.** Cultivating disaffection, lamentations and susceptibilities.
3. **Revenge.** Maintaining ideas of jealousy and urges for revenge.

Incivility. In general, the form of disagreement is what causes misunderstandings, when dissidence is based on incivility, rudeness or evolutionary inexperience.

Separation. Not rarely, it is very difficult for a rude intraphysical consciousness to maintain an adequate level of team spirit in a work group .

Rudeness. In these cases of rudeness, it can be much better that a person leaves for both parties: for the one who leaves and for those who stay.

Help. Thus, we can conclude that not all dissidence is negative but is, in many cases, just the opposite, serving as a source of aid for the continuation of a greater work and the diffusion of leading-edge relative truths that are in development.

WE CAN CONSTANTLY DISAGREE WITH AN INTRAPHYSICAL CONSCIOUSNESS AND, AT THE SAME TIME, COOPERATE AND LEARN MUCH FROM HIM OR HER.

Binomial. The binomial admiration-disagreement is the posture of an intraphysical consciousness who is mature regarding consciential evolution, who knows how to live in peaceful coexistence with another, and whom he or she loves, admires and, at the same time, does not agree always or 100% with that other's points of view, opinions or positions.

Ambiguity. Along with this binomial admiration-disagreement occurs the cosmoethic ambiguity of the *intelligent union of opposites*, a natural and advanced openness for the experience of universalism and maxi-fraternity.

Discrimination. We cannot live with holomaturity if we radically discriminate against certain intraphysical consciousnesses, who are pre-serenissimus and still as imperfect as we are, *always* being 100% in favor of some individuals and 100% against others.

Infantile. This posture characterizes the extreme and definitive dissidence of obstinacy that lacks universalism, in the manner of a preemptive affirmation of infantile regression: "Either we play my way, or I won't play anymore."

Admiration. An intraphysical consciousness who has the greatest fraternal comprehension for someone can love and admire that individual, while also imposing restrictions upon and not always agreeing with them, without incurring any spurious, anti-cosmoethic ambiguity or *indecisiveness*.

Research. The processes of debates, inquiries, refutations and rational research of conscientiology – leading-edge relative truths – demand the refined posture of living the *peaceful coexistence* of the binomial admiration-disagreement, on the part of the conscientiologist.

Institution. In the processes of ideological dissidence within a conscientiocentric institution, where one strives towards leading-edge relative truths, the clarification task and polykarmality, it is important to consider 2 types of disagreement:

A. **Individual.** Individual disagreement.
B. **Group.** Group disagreement.

In individual dissidence, we can point out the dissident who is professional, anti-cosmoethical, mercantilistic and has no team spirit.

Spy. The professional dissident who gets close to and interacts with a scientific institution, for example – in the manner of an industrial spy – with the singular objective of becoming informed or appropriating its curriculum and techniques and, later, creating or adapting, in his or her own way, an institution, that is generally centered around the person or *ego* (maxi-piece or maxi-cog, as opposed to mini-cog), competing with and depreciating the original institution, thus *sullying the plate from which they have eaten*.

Consequences. *Group dissidence* is capable of generating existential mini-programs and existential maxi-programs on an individual or group level, as well as individual or group existential anti-programs and existential incompletism, and triggering group-karmic inseparability.

Categories. Group dissidence can be classified in at least 3 categories:

A. **Marriage.** When a husband decides to leave a team and his wife goes with him, or vice-versa.
B. **Progeny.** When an individual leaves and his or her mother, father, or both, follow together.
C. **Society.** When someone associates with another collaborator in order to form a society and the 2 members leave.

Qualification. We can also classify dissidence into 2 categories, in terms of its extent and qualification: mini and maxi-dissidence.

A. **Mini-dissidence.** Mini-dissidence is provoked by the intraphysical consciousness' *limitation* in terms of his or her acceptance and practice of leading-edge relative truths, exposing personal impotence or incompetence. This is a restricted ideological dissidence.
B. **Maxi-dissidence.** Maxi-dissidence is generated by a *greater renovation* of the intraphysical consciousness, who finds him or herself situated above the average level of the evolutionary work team. This is a broader ideological dissidence.

HE OR SHE WHO REMAINS ALONE OR ISOLATED BECAUSE THEY WISH TO, MAY BE PRACTICING, AT THE VERY LEAST, THE VICE OF OMISSION.

20. EXISTENTIAL PROGRAM AND MINI-DISSIDENCE

Limit. Mini-dissidence in a work team shows the maximum limit of the intraphysical consciousness' possible realizations in his or her current human context, within the existential program, or *mini*-program.

Pressure. In this context, the human personality does not have the capacity to withstand the pressure experienced due to the body of new ideas or the recycle-provoking renovations in his or her life.

Egocentricity. An example of mini-dissidence is that generated by the cosmoethic, which demands that a still egocentric, evolutionarily infantile intraphysical consciousness live with team spirit.

Mini-mechanism. This egocentric intraphysical consciousness becomes his or her own staff of one – a maxi-piece or a mini-mechanism. Unable to endure the renovation, they separate from the group in order to cultivate his or her own exaggerated ego.

IDEOLOGICAL MINI-DISSIDENCE CAN BE: REGRESSIVE OR SELF-MIMICKING AND STATIONARY OR STAGNATING.

Syndrome. *Regressive* mini-dissidence leads one to the Swedenborg syndrome, leaving, for example, a rational, scientific or mentalsomatic path in order to embrace some mystical task, restricted to the belly-brain.

Breadth. *Stationary* mini-dissidence is that of the individual who leaves a team that is researching leading-edge relative truths in order to complacently perform only what they were able to understand, assimilate and endure, within the limits of his or her *evolutionary breadth* or personalism.

Clarification task. An example of maxi-dissidence is the conscious and *healthy* departure of an intraphysical consciousness from a group that is performing sectarian consolation tasks in order to apply their efforts together with another team that performs universalistic clarification tasks, in the execution of an existential *maxi*-program.

Progressive. In ideological maxi-dissidence, which is always progressive or evolutionary, the intraphysical consciousness seeks to practice leading-edge relative truths.

Realities. Leading-edge realities are always refutable and ephemeral, thus not permitting the intraphysical consciousness to regress or become stationary in any determinate part of his or her evolutionary path, if they do not wish to.

Self-corruption. In the execution of the clarification task in group, the dissident separates due to a well defined and specific limitation in each case, almost always in order to not have to confront and eradicate old anti-cosmoethical self-corruption.

Cross-road. The healthy dissident, in an existential maxi-program, chooses another direction upon encountering a cross road in a lazy and carefree intraphysical life, preferring a laborious and organized multidimensional life.

THE MINI-DISSIDENTS WHO FALL INTO ANTIQUATED AND DISPENSABLE SELF-MIMICRY FOSSILIZE THEMSELVES IN EXISTENTIAL INCOMPLETISM.

Conscientiocentrism. The more correct a conscientiocentric institution is, the more it will accentuate 2 opposing facts within itself, in terms of collaborators and mini-dissidents:

A. **Collaborator.** It is very easy to encounter a sickly collaborator.

B. **Mini-dissident.** It is very difficult to find a relatively healthy mini-dissident.

Comparison. Let us seek to instructively compare 2 opposites.

Maxi-mechanism. The following are profile traits of the healthy collaborator:

A. **Integration.** Seeks integral leading-edge relative truths.

B. **Poly-karmality.** Exhibits an ego that is predominately poly-karmic.

C. **Mini-piece.** Transforms him or herself into a *mini*-piece (cog) within an assistential *maxi*-mechanism.

D. **Assistentiality.** Shows a predisposition for being an *intraphysical helper.*

E. **Cosmoethic.** Lives sincerely, with the cosmoethic in the *fore* of his or her assistential service.

F. **Groupality.** Presents the authentic experience of team spirit within a *well-administrated existential program.*

Mini-mechanism. The following are profile traits of the somewhat ill mini-dissident:

A. **Limitation.** Predominately ego-karmic; is partisan of leading-edge relative truths limited by desires (apriorism and preconceptions).

B. **Ego-karmality.** Evidences an *inflated ego* that is equal to or greater than the component egos of the team.

C. **Maxi-piece.** Transforms him or herself into a *maxi*-piece within an assistential *mini*-mechanism.

D. **Intrudability.** Exhibits a predisposition towards being an *intraphysical intruder.*

E. **Anti-cosmoethical.** Covertly lives an anti-cosmoethical life, seeking a *life in the peace of the desert.*

F. **Ectopia.** Develops an exalted egocentric behavior in an *ectopic existential program.*

THE COSMOETHIC DOES NOT LIMIT ACTIONS THAT ARE JUST AND CORRECT. THOSE CONSCIOUSNESSES WHO ARE FREER ARE THE SLAVES OF THE COSMOETHIC.

21. CONSCIENTIAL TRI-ENDOWMENT

Definition. *Intraconsciential tri-endowment* is the quality of bringing together the 3 talents that are most useful to the conscientiologist: intellectuality, parapsychism and communicability, in that order.

Synonymy. An expression equivalent to *intraconsciential tri-endowment: consciential triple- endowment.*

EVERYONE HAS AT LEAST 11 TYPES OF INTELLIGENCE THAT CAN BE DEVELOPED IN LIFE ON EARTH.

Types. Following is a list of the 11 basic intelligences of the human being:

1. **Communicative.**
2. **Contextual.**
3. **Corporal.**
4. **Experimental.**
5. **Internal.**
6. **Linguistic.**
7. **Logical.**
8. **Musical.**
9. **Parapsychic.**
10. **Personal.**
11. **Spatial.**

Aptitudes. Every personality that is more lucid has to look for, identify and develop his or her strong traits, and ascertain which intelligence(s) should be put to use in order to execute the existential program.

Sterile. In physical life there are sterile consciousnesses who do not develop any talent and live very comfortable and accomplished lives, in evolutionary mediocrity, as satisfied robots in *existential robotization*.

Existential robotization. A previous, instinctive or unconscious existential programming – lacking a lucid existential program – generally makes a vulgar intraphysical consciousness into one more animal or evolutionary automaton.

Evolutionology. The victim of existential robotization ignores his or her consciential evolutionary level and is not aware of the details and plans of the evolutionary file that was arranged with the evolutionologist or evolutionary orientor.

Precarious. Unfortunately, this precarious condition of existential robotization still predominates in contemporary humanity that consists of 5 billion 700 million human beings (1996).

THE MAJORITY OF CITIZENS STILL EXHIBIT ONLY ONE NOTABLE TALENT, BEING MERELY CONSCIENTIALLY MONO-ENDOWED.

Celebrated. Some of these mono-endowed persons, having developed only one intelligence, arrive at enormous notoriety; some even become highly celebrated individuals or giants in human history.

Tri-endowed. Still others seek to develop more than one talent, which brings out underlying attributes in innate or inherent multi-millenary and para-genetic versatility, sometimes even achieving consciential tri-endowment.

Collaborators. The International Institute of Projectiology and Conscientiology continues to seek, identify and invite those personalities with potential for super-endowment, capable of employing up to 3 intelligences simultaneously, to be IIPC collaborators.

Consciousness. In all its years of operation, IIPC has sought to select *tri-endowed consciousnesses*, because they are more able to run its departments of administration, education, itinerancy and research of *consciousness per se*.

Evolution. There are 3 intelligences that are more practical for the dynamics of consciousness' evolution, at our current evolutionary levels, that we look for, being formative of tri-endowment: intellectuality or internal intelligence; parapsychism; and communicability.

Which types of intelligence do you recognize as being more developed? What is your greatest intelligence?

22. INTELLECTUALITY IN THE EXISTENTIAL PROGRAM

NO HUMAN EDUCATION IS COMPLETE WITHOUT FULL SELF-AWARENESS OF THE PRIMARY GOALS OF ONE'S OWN EXISTENTIAL PROGRAM.

Essential. A superior intellect is not everything. Of what value is *intellectual brilliance* if an intraphysical consciousness fails disastrously in the essentials of his or her own evolution? Is it worth being a Nobel prize laureate who creates missiles?

Variables. In the amplification of intellectuality or the *serious* investment in personal, general and multi-disciplinary culture, we must intelligently address the following 8 variables of personality:

- A. **Career.** A professional career.
- B. **Diploma.** A formal diploma.
- C. **Polyglotism.** Polyglotism.
- D. **Self-education.** Self-education.
- E. **Library.** A personal library.
- F. **Self-scrutiny.** Self-scrutiny.
- G. **Hetero-scrutiny.** Hetero-scrutiny.
- H. **Artifacts.** The essential artifacts of knowledge.

University. For the youth who is keenly aware of existential inversion and the existential program, university life is merely a rite of passage between one transitory intraphysical condition and another of greater intraphysical consciential maturity.

Research. In school, youths will try to learn how to learn, to study the method of study, to amplify the cerebral dictionary in order to access the holo-memory, and create inventions by researching original ideas.

Career. Above all, the university student will seek to obtain a diploma in order to establish a career and become a competent professional.

Corporatism. It is most intelligent for the young student of consciousness not to expose him or herself too much, in order to not create problems for him or herself. It is also best not to become too deeply engaged in the superficial and transitory movements that exist within the university holothosene.

Seduction. These movements attempt to seduce and involve the promising youth with the useless attempt to renew the unrenewable, when the issues are stratified in the politics, philosophy and blind corporatism of a conventional university.

Conscientiality. The youth's mentality or conscientiality should allow him or her to rise above this period of formal study, in preparation for the execution of his or her more advanced existential program, without concerning him or her about proselytizing or indoctrinating new friends.

Paradigms. While a student, the defense of paradigm shifts, with narrow-minded or fossilized professionals for example, becomes secondary.

Diploma. These (paradigm shifts) should be developed with dedication, after graduation, with diploma in hand and professional authority having been conquered through work experience.

EVEN WITHOUT BEING CERTAIN OF ANYTHING, UNSATISFIED WITH ITSELF AND CONSTANTLY RECREATING ITSELF, SCIENCE PROGRESSES.

Stigmas. It is important, in the existential program, to consider the formal education of intraphysical consciousness, keeping in mind 2 stigmas that can be generated by a university education, and which should be avoided:

A. **Dropping out.** Dropping out of a basic program that has been started, whether in the beginning or the middle of accrued university credits, with the subsequent loss of opportunities for the rest of one's human life, creating a stigma of inferiority and inefficiency.

B. **Superiority.** The intraphysical consciousness who obtains a diploma and is stigmatized by the pragmatic, intraphysical superiority of professional standing and economic productivity in the face of evolved development of conscientiality, the clarification task and poly-karmality.

Self-education. Aside from all the preceding considerations, what matters most is the lifelong, uninterrupted self-education of the existential program's executor, with the intention of staying up-to-date and theorical (theory + practice) in terms of advanced knowledge in his or her area.

Reading. Self-education implies the maintenance of uninterrupted, varied research and selective reading over a period of decades.

Polyglotism. In the intellectuality of the existential program, the intraphysical conscious will ideally know 2 languages, aside from his or her native tongue.

Language. We should opt to be universalistic and polyglots, without ignoring the cultivation of our native language.

Dictionary. We will always have a richer, more dynamic cerebral dictionary in our native tongue, as a function of genetics and the social-cultural-environmental influences that act on and in our consciential micro-universe.

Library. The library is a place where the common, *hurried* person's time is *wasted*.

THERE ARE 1-DAY BOOKS WRITTEN FOR BOOKSTORES. THERE ARE 1-CENTURY BOOKS THAT WERE WRITTEN FOR LIBRARY CONSULTATION.

Abnegation. Sincerity, authenticity, honesty and abnegation are the simple and most intelligent conditions that allow a consciousness to proceed in his or her evolution and the completion of the existential program.

Conduct. There is a fundamental cosmoethical rule of conduct that is valid for regulating the preliminary principles of mega-fraternity: *do not allow yourself to be manipulated and do not manipulate other consciousnesses.*

Scrutiny. Knowledge can only progress through criticism, or rather: self-scrutiny and hetero-scrutiny.

Self-scrutiny. Self-scrutiny permits an intraphysical consciousness to eliminate self-corruption and bad intentions in the current existence. This provides a firm foundation for the adequate execution of the existential program.

Bad intentions. Bad intentions, *the intention to damage someone,* or the conscious, self-corrupt and anti-cosmoethical act, brings the perpetrator a series of at least 5 *holo-karmic pressures*, in the following chronological order:

A. **Suspicion:** remorse, ego-karma.
B. **Rumor:** various types of criticism.
C. **Public opinion:** persecution, parapsychic mishaps.
D. **Accusations:** conscientization, intraphysical melancholy.
E. **Justice:** atonement, group-karma.

Hetero-scrutiny. The value of the conscientiologist's work performed with leading-edge relative truths can be measured by the vigor, frequency and quantity of hetero-scrutiny they receive.

ONE SINCERE HETERO-SCRUTINY (BITING COMMENTARY) *IS WORTH* MORE THAN *1,000* PRAISES (HOT AIR) FOR OUR EVOLUTION.

Neo-synapses. A reduction in hetero-scrutiny shows that one is neither creating nor disseminating new ideas that are capable of generating new evolutionarily libertarian synapses.

Growth. The absence of hetero-scrutiny generates no growing crises, which otherwise occur due to the healthy stressing of the ideological self-defenses of those predisposed targeted individuals.

Artifacts. We can point out 12 categories for the multiple artifacts of knowledge or the mentalsomatic tools of the existential program's executor:

A. **Books.**
B. **Diskettes. (CD-ROMs).**
C. **Personal organizer.**
D. **Diary of experiences.**
E. **Reference books.**
F. **Dictionaries.**
G. **Encyclopedias.**
H. **Periodicals.**
I. **Clippings.**
J. *E-mail.*
K. **Multimedia.**
L. **Files** in one's personal *notebook computer.*

NOT RARELY, ONE REFERENCE BOOK IS WORTH A LIBRARY SHELF FULL OF BOOKS.

Dictionary. A dictionary of similar or analogous ideas overcomes the failures of hypomnesia or a weak memory. It is ideal to acquire the habit of consulting one regularly in our intellectual work.

Bio-memory. The analog dictionary is an aid to the mentalsoma's attributes, an annexation or optional peripheral of the bio-memory, the restricted memory of our cerebrum.

Youths. All dictionaries should be emphatically dedicated, above all, to youths.

Mini-vocabulary. The cerebral memory of young men and women still have smaller lexical units – or only a mini-vocabulary.

Reserve. It is ideal for the intraphysical consciousness to maintain a reserve of consciential potentialities (consciential micro-universe) in order to maintain holosomatic homeostasis.

Prevention. An opportune reserve of mentalsomatic potentialities avoids mental stress, *surmenage*, nervous breakdown, blockages and bioenergetic imbalances.

Percentage. In the execution of the existential program, it is best to use up to 90% of the one's possible consciential attributes, always knowing how and when to use (or not to use) them.

Attributes. The consciential attributes mentioned here, are the elaboration of thought, memory, imagination, and the association and comparison of ideas.

THE SLAVES OF THE ORTHODOXY IN VOGUE, OR THE FADS OF INTRAPHYSICAL SOCIETY, DO NOT EVOLVE IN EXISTENTIAL PROGRAMOLOGY.

23. MENTALSOMATICS

Mentalsomatics. Mentalsomatics *(mental + soma + tics)* is the area of specialization in conscientiology that studies the mentalsoma, the para-body of discernment.

Existential maxi-program. Intellectuality (mentalsomatics) is of primary importance in modern life, and notably, in the execution of the existential program of any consciousness, particularly when this individual develops an existential maxi-program.

THE TRINOMIAL RATIONALITY-DISCERNMENT- HOLOMATURITY REPRESENTS HOMEOSTASIS IN THE EMPLOYMENT OF THE MENTALSOMA.

Foundation. This mentalsomatic trinomial is the ideal foundation for all major decisions, the time line and execution of the lucid intraphysical consciousness' existential program, serving to open the path for existential completism and existential moratorium.

Periods. The development of personal mentalsomatics, in an intraphysical life, can be divided into 2 distinct and inevitable chronological periods:

A. **Acquisition.** Intellectual acquisition or mentalsomatic sowing.
B. *Harvesting. Intellectual reaping* or mentalsomatic harvesting.

Sowing. At first, the young intraphysical consciousness (consciential restriction – see glossary) works on making acquisitions (sowing) in the preparatory phase of the existential program, with only 10%, for example, of his or her own knowledge (para-genetics, potentialities, innate ideas).

Holo-archive. In this case, the youth utilizes 90% of his or her holo-archive (compilation of information from artifacts of knowledge), still in formation, which they seek to diligently compose, transferring his or her findings and research to the mentalsoma's permanent files daily.

Harvesting. After decades of heavy cultural investment, now in the execution phase of the intraphysical program, the mature intraphysical consciousness (having hyperacuity) works to *harvest* his or her intellectual fruits, with 90% of his or her resources (intraphysical memory, cerebral dictionary, holomemory, association of ideas).

Artifacts. In the acquisition phase, the mature individual utilizes only 10% of his or her holo-archive, composed of thousands of *artifacts of knowledge*, which have been transferred to the mentalsoma and are almost indispensable.

Lucidity. In this context, two forms of interconnection occur with lucid intraphysical consciousnesses between existential inversion and penta:

A. **Existential inversion.** Intellectual acquisition – investment in oneself – is the intraphysical period dominated by existential inversion.

B. **Penta.** Intellectual *reaping* – harvesting performed in favor of others – is the intraphysical period dominated by penta.

Strong **traits.** Upon the attainment of the above-mentioned requisites, it is important to consider the natural acquisition of 4 *strong* traits:

A. **Synthesis.** Reasonable powers of intellectual synthesis.

B. **Heuristic.** The development of a heuristic sense of originality.

C. **Curiosity.** A healthy curiosity that is characteristic of science.

D. **Picturesqueness.** *Feeling* regarding picturesqueness.

ALL FACTIOUS HUMAN DOCTRINES, WITHOUT EXCEPTION, ARE LEASHES FOR THE EGO THAT STRAIGHT-JACKET THE MENTALSOMA.

24. PSYCHIC CAPACITIES IN THE EXISTENTIAL PROGRAM

Para-perceptions. All persons possess some degree of energetic and parapsychic perceptions. These para-perceptions are capable of being consciously and voluntarily developed, without limits.

Instrument. Parapsychism (psychic capacities), when developed in a healthy manner, only helps the individual, like an additional instrument, in the intra and extraphysical progress, including the execution of any type of existential program.

Past. If, in the current life, an intraphysical consciousness feels more self-realized with the existential program, he or she does not enjoy dwelling upon the details of his or her previous life. They remember it, however, and are capable of researching it using retrocognitions that include past experiences which are discordant with current ones.

Prioritization. It is extremely important to prioritize the best and most current items in our evolutionary path.

Approaches. In the development of para-psychism, we need to address the following 4 fundamental variables:

1. **VS.** Vibrational state (VS).
2. **Cosmoethic.** The cosmoethic.
3. **De-intrudability.** Freedom from intrusion.
4. **Penta.** Penta (personal energetic task).

THE VIBRATIONAL STATE IS THE TECHNIQUE FOR MAXIMALLY ACCELERATING THE ENERGIES OF THE HOLOCHAKRA, THROUGH THE IMPULSE OF THE WILL.

Cosmoethic. The cosmoethic *(cosmo + ethic)* is that ethic or reflection upon the multi-dimensional cosmic morality that defines consciential holomaturity, which is beyond intraphysical social morality and that which is exhibited by any human labels or categories.

IN FREEDOM FROM INTERCONSCIENTIAL INTRUSION, WE MUST ADDRESS FREEDOM FROM SELF-INTRUSION AND FROM HETERO-INTRUSION.

Penta. Penta *(p + en + ta)* is the daily, multi-dimensional personal energetic task that involves the permanent assistance of the helpers and the technical transmission of consciential energies (CEs), by a human consciousness (intraphysical consciousness), directly to extraphysical consciousnesses or projected consciousnesses.

Clauses. The penta practice is highly discipline producing, being performed in the waking state and without intraphysical witnesses.

Mega-challenge. The most challenging aspect of the penta practice is that it is performed for the rest of the practitioner's human life.

Assistance. Through assistance to others, the intraphysical consciousness can regulate the bases of support for the completion of the existential program's clauses, regardless of its nature.

Prevention. Some talents are ideally suited for the facilitation of the intraphysical consciousness' capacity to withstand the mishaps, interconsciential intrusions and intrusive stigmas that are eventual and inevitable in this still pathological intraphysical society.

***Strong* traits.** Following are 6 *strong* traits that are specifically suited for the practicing of continued, communicative, assistential parapsychism:

A. **Veteran.** The practice of penta by someone – a man or woman – who is mature and a veteran of life.

B. **Universalism.** A temperament that allows the intraphysical consciousness to live without discriminating against others and to have an advanced universalist spirit, without an autocratic character.

C. **Health.** Enjoy a relatively prolonged state of good health.

D. **Family.** Have an adequate family life, with relative personal independence.

E. **Affectivity.** Maintain a stable monogamous affective-sex life devoid of chronic deficiency.

F. **Scholarship.** Not be depending on formal or university studies that are unfinished.

THERE IS A CRITICAL POINT AT WHICH INTRUDABILITY BECOMES UNBEARABLE AND THE INTRUDER CEASES ANTI-COSMOETHICAL PRACTICES.

25. CONSCIENTIAL ENERGIES

Definition. The *holochakra (holo + chakra)* is the energetic para-body of consciousness (intraphysical consciousness).

Synonymy. The following 3 expressions are equivalent to *holochakra:*

A. *Bioplasmic para-body.*
B. *Counter-body.*
C. *Energetic para-body.*

THE UNDERSTANDING AND LUCID USE OF ONE'S HOLOCHAKRA SHOULD BE A PRIORITY AT OUR CURRENT EVOLUTIONARY LEVEL.

Energy. Consciential energy (CE) is that immanent (cosmic) energy which consciousness employs in general manifestations.
Ene. Consciential energy comprises the *ene* of thosene.
Flexibility. Consciential energy possesses characteristics that need to be clearly distinguished by the intraphysical consciousness in order for him or her to develop a greater holochakral flexibility.

Characteristics. Following are 10 categories of consciential energies, according to their specific characteristics:

A. **Source:** will, consciousness, decision, origination of flow.
B. **Potency:** intensity, pressure, and intelligent control of energy.
C. **Rhythm:** intermittent flow, continuous flow.
D. **Dynamic:** movement, instability and velocity of flow.

E. **Direction:** perception, directed transmission, directed reception.
F. **Object:** person, cure, hostility, aggressivity.
G. **Target:** specific location, particular organ.
H. **Quality:** agreeable, disagreeable; healthy, sick; curative, illness causing; defensive, attacking.
I. **Lucidity:** unconscious, semi-conscious, conscious.
J. **Supply:** intermittent, continuous (pregnant mother – fetus).

Conscientization. Conscientization of the methodology, classification and manners of employment of consciential energies helps greatly in the improvement of intra and extraphysical assistance that we seek to offer other consciousnesses in the execution of our existential programs.

Bioenergetics. According to bioenergetics (consciential or personal energies), intraphysical consciousnesses can be classified into 6 categories, for example, in terms of the donation and reception of energetic flows:

A. **Balance.** Balanced, positive donors (health).
B. **Unbalance.** Unbalanced negative donors.
C. **Vampirization.** Vampirizing, negative receivers.
D. **Blockages.** Blocked positive receivers.
E. **Egoism.** Egoistic closed and defensive.
F. **Unconscious.** Unconscious neutralizers.

Health. As you can see, only the first category is reasonably healthy. The others present some manner of restriction that is often not perceived and undetected, in terms of consciential balance.

NO ONE KNOWS EXACTLY WHEN THEY WILL NEED TO EMPLOY AN EMERGENCY INTERDIMENSIONAL ENERGETIC RESOURCE.

Scholarship. An illiterate person can be a good artisan or competently perform a manual task.

AN INTRAPHYSICAL CONSCIOUSNESS WITH LITTLE EDUCATION CAN MASTER HIS OR HER OWN CONSCIENTIAL ENERGIES, INDEPENDENT OF HAVING LIMITED KNOWLEDGE.

Space-time. Strictly speaking, consciential energy is not influenced by the factors of time or space, or rather, of space-time.

Conditioning. However, the reactions of our personal psychology, our repressions and conditioning ideas, influence our experiences with energies.

Loss. The loss of the use of consciential energy is the same as the loss of time or opportunities that have already passed.

Discipline. It is best that the intraphysical consciousness better organize him or herself, with the intention of applying energies more usefully from now on.

Energetic springtime. Energetic springtime is a fairly long-lasting personal condition characterized by maximally healthy and constructive consciential energies.

Duo. *Energetic springtime for two* is the energetic springtime of the evolutionary duo, who truly love each other and have mastered the applications of healthy consciential energies, with complete lucidity.

Acceleration. Energetic springtime *by two* accelerates the execution of the existential programs *of the two* partners composing an evolutionary duo, through consciential gestations *by two*.

Penta. If a novice penta practitioner exteriorizes consciential energies 25 times per minute, during 50 minutes, he or she will achieve at least 1,250 exteriorizations per day.

Decade. With the continuation of this task over time, he or she will achieve a total of 37,500 exteriorizations per month;

450,000 exteriorizations per year; and 4,500,000 exteriorizations in a decade.

Soma. This fact illustrates that the soma is a powerful machine for the exteriorization of preventative and therapeutic energies. This helps enormously in the execution of any type of existential program.

Let's donate our consciential energy as we would throw a cup of water into the sea: always contribute, even if only a small amount.

26. COMMUNICABILITY IN THE EXISTENTIAL PROGRAM

WITHOUT INTERCONSCIENTIAL COMMUNICATION, EVOLUTION OF CONSCIOUSNESS IS NOT POSSIBLE.

Era. We currently live in an era of interconsciential communication, the likes of which has never occurred with mankind in any epoch of society.

Fossilization. He or she who does not communicate becomes fossilized in his or her own egocentricity (ego-karma), in any sector of human inquiry.

Complexity. The completion of any existential program becomes impracticable without communicability, which is becoming progressively more complex.

Manners. Intraphysical consciousness' broader communicability can become amplified in the following 4 manners:

1. **Writing.** In writing, we cannot forget imaging, discourse and analysis – intellectual processes that are currently used with the aid of a personal *notebook computer.*

2. **Speaking.** In speaking, it is important to emphasize warmth, colloquialisms, eloquence and rhetoric.

3. **Bioenergetics.** In bioenergetics it is important to consider the processes of energy during classes, energy fields and interconsciential self-defense.

4. **Parapsychism.** In parapsychism it its important to highlight pangraphy (sophisticated multi-modal automatic writing) and lucid projectability.

Science. What quality is better for directing our existential program: communication through art or through science?

Art. Generally speaking, working in the different areas of art – including the plastic arts, film, photography, literature, music, theater and television – can merely be an escape on the part of the intraphysical consciousness from the execution of his or her true, more demanding and laborious, existential program.

ART CAN REPRESENT DISPENSABLE SELF-MIMICRY AND AN ECTOPIC SELF-RELAY FOR THE INTRAPHYSICAL CONSCIOUSNESS.

Utilization. The same effort, time, energies and thosenes that we invest in artistic messages are better utilized and offer more productive results in our evolutionary acceleration with scientific research.

27. COMMUNICATIVE PROJECTABILITY

States. Certain altered states of consciousness, including healthy retrocognitions, can offer precise and precious indications that allow the intraphysical consciousness to identify and discover the details of his or her existential program and amplify interconsciential communicability.

THE THEORICE (THEORY + PRACTICE) OF PROJECTIOLOGY IS AN EXTRAORDINARY RESOURCE FOR DEEPLY UNDERSTANDING OUR EXISTENTIAL PROGRAMS.

Projectability. The ideal, for the recollection of one's existential program, is to develop the processes of conscious projection, provoke the expansion of lucid consciousness while outside the body, access one's holo-memory and install healthy retrocognitions.

Channeling. Can human intermediation, mediumship or channeling between consciential dimensions be executed on a scientific basis? Clearly it can.

Interference. Nevertheless, it is extremely difficult to obtain mediumship of an adequately trustworthy level, due to the many points of emotional interference between extraphysical and intraphysical consciousnesses.

Mystification. The emotions of the intermediary between intraphysical and extraphysical consciousnesses favors self-corruption, mystification and manipulation of needy intraphysical consciousnesses, with political designs, or secretive or anti-cosmoethical motives of group domination.

Fascination. In the end, anti-cosmoethical mediumship predisposes something even worse: fascination of a group of individuals who are exploited and abused by religions and sects having mediumistic and syncretic foundations.

Reliability. It is possible that, in the future, we will find a more reliable process of intermediation between the consciential dimensions, beyond vulgar intraphysical consciousnesses or physical instruments, machines and fallible and manipulatable apparatuses.

Today. So far, individual lucid projectability still presents fewer errors in multidimensional communicability for the motivated intraphysical consciousness.

UPON BEING REBORN, CONSCIOUSNESS EXHIBITS A DISCARDABLE CONTAINER *(SOMA)* AND AN ESSENCE THAT IS ALWAYS "RETURNABLE" *(CONSCIOUSNESS).*

28. EXISTENTIAL PROGRAM AND TIME

Assistance. How do you, experimenter, spend your time in intraphysical life: In assistance towards others, or only on yourself?

Time. When analyzing what is useful for us in terms of the evolutionary path, it is important to attentively consider the factor of time.

Clarification task. Time is an evolved condition, when we understand it well. It is a variable that is much more healthy than harmful, because it satisfactorily executes the clarification task upon us.

Cure. Time, silence and de-soma (biological death) cure all intraphysical disturbances.

Minute. The value of a minute (time) is the qualitative intensity of the experience for any consciousness.

Evolution. In terms of consciential evolution, 5 minutes can be worth 1 decade.

Age. Five minutes in the life of a 20-year-old intraphysical consciousness do not have the same value as 5 minutes, when that same intraphysical consciousness is 60 years old.

Phases. Five minutes lived during the preparatory phase of one's human life or existential program, from 1 to 35 years of age, for example, do not have the same value or weight as 5 minutes lived by the same intraphysical consciousness in the execution phase, from 36 to 70 years of age.

Evaluation. It is always important to evaluate whether our 5 minutes are currently really worth 5 minutes, or if they are worth less or more than this.

ACCORDING TO CONSCIENTIOLOGY, TIME IS A UNIT OF EVOLUTIONARY MEASURE THAT IS VALUABLE AND USEFUL FOR THE LUCID CONSCIOUSNESS.

Self-organization. The ambiguity of time demands that we establish a solid behavior-pattern in order to take advantage of the uniformity of minutes. Evolutionary self-organization arises from this.

Condition. An existential condition, or even a personal posture, can be useful, adequate and fine today, but entirely outdated, negative or harmful for ourself and others tomorrow.

Foresight. Only our foresight, with a unified vision in terms of space and time, can accelerate the correct execution of our existential program.

THE PAST-PRESENT *IS THE* EVOLUTIONARY MOMENT OF NEOPHOBES. *THE* PRESENT-FUTURE *IS THE* EVOLUTIONARY MOMENT OF NEOPHILES.

Present. A child lives in the present, in order to survive by breathing, in a condition imposed by implacable intraphysical restriction.

Infancy. Infancy is the period in which the worst coercion is exercised upon consciousness by human life, when the individual is in the preparatory phase for the execution of the existential program.

Future. The adult (woman or man) lives in the future, because the present is already his or her immediate future.

Maturity. Having already recuperated a greater number of units of lucidity (cons) and being prepared for the execution of the existential program, the adult lives at the apex of his or her holomaturity.

Cons. It is important to emphasize that, for the majority of intraphysical consciousnesses, the accessing of one's personal existential program depends on a reasonable recuperation of cons.

Holomaturity. Holomaturity joins together 5 relevant factors:

1. **Biology.** The biological maturity of your soma.

2. **Psychology.** The psychological maturity of your current brain.
3. **Integral.** The integral development of your holo-memory.
4. **Intelligences.** The multiple intelligences that you possess.
5. **Egos.** The well-defined employment of your egos.

MANY PEOPLE OF ADVANCED AGE LIVE IN THE PAST, BEING PREDOMINATELY LUCID ABOUT RECOLLECTIONS OR NOSTALGIC ABOUT THE PAST.

Fruits. Already having either completed the existential program or not (existential completism or incompletism, existential moratorium or intraphysical melancholy), an older person prepares to gather the fruits of his or her efforts from yet another step taken in Earth's school-hospital, in a new post-de-somatic intermissive period.

Consciential epicenter. An intraphysical consciousness who has achieved the state of being permanently-totally-intrusion-free or being a lucid consciential epicenter simultaneously lives, regardless of age, in the following 3 time frames with the 3 accompanying parapsychic implications:

A. **Past:** retrocognitions.
B. **Present:** simul-cognitions or parapsychic knowledge of facts that occur at the exact moment, but at a distance from the perceiver.
C. **Future:** precognitions.

Trinomial. The trinomial re-somas-retrocognitions-precognitions is the most effective process for the evolutionary acceleration of our re-somas (physical rebirths) in series (existential series), within the personal multi-existential cycle.

Retrocognitions. Healthy, multiple, consecutive and *cultural* retrocognitions (past life recall), aid the intraphysical consciousness to open, within him or herself, an ample intraconsciential universe, upon distinguishing characteristic details of the diverse egos and intelligences that they have assumed. This can occur in different areas, through the millenniums, similar to the following 14:

    A. **Anthropology.** Human bodies (anthropology).
    B. **Sexo-somatics.** Both human genders (sexology).
    C. **Eugenics.** The human species (eugenics).
    D. **Genetics.** Genetic inheritance (genetics).
    E. **Para-genetics.** Personal inheritance (para-genetics).
    F. **Sociology.** Social groups (sociology).
    G. **Geography.** Locations (human geography).
    H. **Culture.** Cultural patrimony (culture).
    I. **Linguistics.** Languages and dialects (linguistics).
    J. **Work.** Professions or occupations (work).
    K. **History.** Epochs (human history).
    L. **De-somatics.** Types of de-somas (de-somatics or thanatology).
    M. **Thosenology.** Mentalities (thosenology).
    N. **Evolutionology.** Evolutionary levels (evolutionology).

Elimination. Retrocognitions, when experienced extraphysically by the projector, for example, facilitate the elimination of 2 inconveniences:

    1. **Existential series.** Instinctual existential series (rebirth cycle) without lucid pre-planning.
    2. **Self-mimicry.** Complacent repetition of dispensable intraphysical experiences (outdated self mimicry), that pour in from our past, through para-genetics .

EVERY INTRAPHYSICAL ENVIRONMENT IS A STAGE FOR DIVERSE MULTI-DIMENSIONAL AUDIENCES, INCLUDING PARA-TROPOSPHERIC EXTRAPHYSICAL CONSCIOUSNESSES.

Precognitions. Extraphysical precognitions, experienced by the projected projector, for example, permit the intraphysical consciousness 2 conquests:

1. **Preparation.** Anticipated awareness, in the here-and-now, of the preparatory details for one's next human existence, within a *planned existential series*.
2. **Future.** The self-aware experiencing of the principle that the present is the immediate *future*, within the execution of the existential program that has been identified and is already being performed.

Self-relay. The repetition (recurrence) of personal specifications, or traits that are peculiar and common to these different egos, permit the intraphysical consciousness to identify, beyond appearances, the basic structural lines of his or her own self-relays in similar consecutive existential programs.

Complexity. The lucid consciential epicenter has diverse memories (holo-memory), employs more than one mode of intelligence (intellectuality, parapsychism, communicability), and participates in various consciential dimensions (multidimensionality).

Mini-piece. It is no longer important to this self-aware human consciential epicenter whether they are intraphysical or extraphysical. They are more concerned with the quality of complex performance as a mini-piece within an assistential and inter-consciential maxi-mechanism.

WHEN WE PROGRAM OURSELVES WITH FORESIGHT, WE DEMONSTRATE OUR MAXIMAL DISCERNMENT RELATIVE TO TIME.

Categories. Strictly speaking, we can rationally classify existential programs into 3 distinct categories, with regards to the time of execution:

1. **On time.** An existential program that is up-to-date, current or on time.
2. **Behind schedule.** An existential program that is behind schedule.
3. **Ahead of schedule.** An existential program that is ahead of schedule.

Recyclers. An existential program that is behind schedule should be attentively considered, particularly by existential recyclers of all types.

Invertors. An existential program that is ahead of schedule should be attentively considered, particularly by lucid existential invertors, as an evolutionary potentiality that is at hand.

THE EXECUTION OF AN EXISTENTIAL PROGRAM CAN BE PERFORMED IN 3 STAGES: SHORT-TERM, MEDIUM-TERM AND LONG-TERM.

| **29.** SHORT-TERM ACCOMPLISHMENTS |

IN EACH STAGE OF COMPLETION OF AN EXISTENTIAL PROGRAM, BOTH PRIMARY AND SECONDARY GOALS SHOULD BE CONSIDERED.

Urgency. In the short-term, it is of primary importance for the intraphysical consciousness to *master the vibrational state.*

Discipline. Without the vibrational state, it becomes difficult to efficiently execute a more advanced existential program with discipline and without spurious interference.

Key. The vibrational state is the energetic key to the intraphysical consciousness' life, which is an indirect, entirely energetic existence that manifests through 2 typically energetic bodies: the holochakra (body of energy) and the soma.

Anticipation. At the level of pre-serenissimus in which the individual finds him or herself, an intraphysical consciousness tries to get as close to the permanently-totally-intrusion-free condition as possible. At this stage it is necessary to plan and do things as much ahead of time as possible in order to achieve the permanently-totally-intrusion-free condition.

30. MEDIUM-TERM ACCOMPLISHMENTS

Practicality. In the minutely detailed medium-term planning of an existential program, practical variables or experiential conditions need to be included, such as the following 3 indispensable goals:

1. **Assistentiality.** The practice of interconsciential assistentiality.
2. **Penta.** The practice of penta (personal energetic task).
3. **Consciential epicenter.** Becoming a lucid consciential epicenter.

ONE CERTAIN AND SOUND BENEFIT IS WORTH MORE THAN 1,000 BENEFITS THAT MAY BECOME LIABILITIES.

31. Long-term Accomplishments

Ambitions. In the long-term phase, in which secondary, but indispensable, goals predominate, one should foresee consciousness' greater, healthy evolutionary ambitions.

Conquests. After much practice, an intraphysical consciousness will be a veteran penta practitioner, have an extraphysical clinic, may have achieved the permanently-totally-intrusion-free condition and have high-quality parapsychic experiences, including projections with continuous consciousness.

Longevity. The average human being is prepared to surpass the 1-century barrier of intraphysical existence, arriving at the last third of life such that the *4-generation family* becomes commonplace: parent, child, grandchild and great grandchild.

AS A RESULT OF HUMAN LONGEVITY, EXISTENTIAL PROGRAMS WILL SOON BE OF PROGRESSIVELY LONGER DURATION.

Strong **traits.** According to current thanatology or desomatics research, the majority of centenarian intraphysical consciousnesses have 3 characteristic *strong* traits:

1. **Harmony.** A sense of harmony.
2. **Will.** Will power.
3. **Adjustment.** A capacity to adjust.

Self-organization. It is worth adding the strong traits of these long-lived individuals to our self-organization, and consequently, to the execution of our existential program during the intraphysical stage *(lifetime)* or in our long-term life accomplishments.

The final result of our existential program can be the achievement of existential completion, incompletion or multi-completion.

32. EXISTENTIAL COMPLETISM

Definition. *Existential completism* is the contentment resulting from satisfactory execution of the behavior, manifestations and works of a human consciousness' existential program, that was planned beforehand during the intermissive period.

Synonymy. Equivalent expressions for *existential completion*: *fulfilled life mission; existential completeness.*

Projects. Existential completism is the crowning achievement of an intraphysical consciousness' total personal efforts and is only accomplished with the good administration of the individual's *life projects*.

Level. A human consciousness is an existential completist if they completed his or her existential program, be it a lesser or greater one, within the correct path, directive, sector and level.

Intraphysical euphoria. Completion of the existential program generates intraphysical euphoria.

Extraphysical euphoria. As well as generating intraphysical euphoria in the individual's life, existential completion can provoke extraphysical euphoria in one's *intermissive life*, after de-soma, in the intermissive period (the extraphysical period between two human lives).

THE ATTAINMENT OF EXISTENTIAL COMPLETION, AT THE END OF HUMAN LIFE, IS A PRE-REQUISITE FOR ENJOYING EXTRAPHYSICAL EUPHORIA IN THE INTERMISSIVE PERIOD.

Demand. Strictly speaking, no one is going to demand satisfaction from an extraphysical consciousness, who has recently left human life, for the failed acts and/or items omitted from the execution of the existential program.

Experience. Within his or her own micro-universe, an extraphysical consciousness senses and experiences at least the following 3 conditions:

A. **Results.** Sees the healthy or pathological results of those things they have done in recent human life.

B. **Thosenity.** Perceives the comfortable or uncomfortable quality of his or her thosenity through his or her energies.

C. **Cosmoethics.** Detects his or her intraconsciential level of cosmoethic.

Self-demands. Thus, intraconsciential self-demands are made.

Hetero-demands. Generalized hetero-demands are not made – except in excessively pathological cases of extraphysical intrusion related to existential incompletists having *executed zero percent* of his or her existential program.

Code. The achievement of existential completion depends on the intraphysical consciousness' relationship with his or her evolutionary group and the constitution of a practical, *personal code of principles* for living on Earth and successfully executing his or her existential program.

Interdependence. Regardless of its inevitability, consciential interdependence should not get in the way of our doing what is necessary in terms of our existential program.

Amounts. Existential completion is not a result of heroic acts, but of small amounts of sacrifice and service in favor of the common good.

Group. Interdependence between intraphysical consciousnesses helps greatly, being indispensable for the realization of group existential programs.

Not transferable. *Groupal existential programs* do not signify transference of existential programs from father to son or mother to daughter. Existential programs are, above all, always specific and not transferable. A natural interdependency, however, occurs between intraphysical consciousnesses, in order for them to live on Earth. *Poly-karmic existential programs* also exist, that depend upon a group of intraphysical consciousnesses.

SOME EXISTENTIAL COMPLETISTS ARE ENTIRELY UNAWARE OF THE EXISTENTIAL MINI-PROGRAM'S CLAUSES.

Instinct. Legions of individuals live and work in a fairly spontaneous manner, without being conscious his or her options, in an automatic and para-instinctive way.

Professionals. Following are 2 examples of common existential completists who are professionals in intraphysical society:

1. **Surgeon.** The successful surgeon with decades of social service rendered.
2. **Writer.** The devoted conventional writer, as an intellectual who has received all awards in his or her field.

Consolation task. Here are 3 well known examples of completists regarding the consolation task:

A. Albert Schweitzer: Protestantism.
B. Mother Theresa: Catholicism.
C. Francisco ("Chico") Cândido Xavier (famous Brazilian medium): Spiritism (New Spiritualism).

IN ORDER TO ACHIEVE EXISTENTIAL COMPLETISM IT IS BEST, FOR EXAMPLE, TO LIVE FOR IDEAS – NOT FOR MONEY.

Half-way. If one is going to do things half-way it will take them twice as long to become an existential completist.

Daily. Day-to-day completism gradually comprises the completism of an entire life.

Prize. The prize of existential completism is to choose a future, better human body – a macro-soma – for the next multi-existential evolutionary period.

Macro-soma. Beyond a certain evolutionary level, the super-customized human body, or macro-soma, is much more intrinsically connected to holo-karmic processes related to the evolutionologist than we can imagine.

Research. Both the macro-soma and evolutionologists merit greater research attention from all of us.

THE ACHIEVEMENT OF EXISTENTIAL COMPLETISM, IN THE PREVIOUS LIFE, IS A NATURAL PRE-REQUISITE FOR THE ACQUISITION OF A MACRO-SOMA, IN THE NEXT LIFE.

Cosmoethic. An intraphysical consciousness only attains existential completion in certain evolved existential programs if they develop an immense cosmoethical, healthy ambition. This ambition acts within one's own consciential micro-universe.

Well-being. The complete realization of the existential program is indisputably relevant to the subjective well-being of the intraphysical consciousness, today, and the extraphysical consciousness, tomorrow.

Directives. Nevertheless, merely knowing the fundamental directives of one's own life is still insufficient and does not predispose this feeling of well-being.

Challenge. For the lucid consciousness, after having achieved at an advanced level of holo-maturity, the challenge of the existential program is much more significant and relevant than the intraphysical euphoria of existential completion.

Question. It is worth the effort for the recycling (see glossary) intraphysical consciousness to ask and respond to the following question: "What do I crave more, the intraphysical euphoria of existential completism, *tomorrow*, or the challenge of executing my existential program, *today?*

Effects. Existential completion generates multiplicative effects on consciential evolution with positive results such as these 6: existential moratorium, existential maxi-moratorium, existential multi-completion, macro-soma, existential maxi-program and the permanently-totally-intrusion-free condition (see glossary).

Trinomial. The *trinomial motivation-effort-perseverance* is an indispensable practical posture for all intraphysical consciousnesses who seek to prioritize the attainment of existential completism.

THE INTELLIGENT EVOLUTIONARY DUO IS COMPOSED IN ORDER FOR THE COUPLE *TO SEEK THE EXECUTION OF* EXISTENTIAL COMPLETISM *TOGETHER.*

33. EXISTENTIAL INCOMPLETISM

Definition. *Existential incompletism* is the frustrating, chronic, uncomfortable condition of incomplete, unsatisfactory execution of the human consciousness' existential program that had been planned during his or her intermissive period.

Synonymy. The following 3 expressions are equivalent to *existential incompletism:*

A. *Evolutionary non-fulfillment (i.e., of contract).*
B. *Existential semi-completion.*
C. *Limited existential completism.*

Maturity. The individual who has not realized his or her existential program, not having succeeded in completing the greater tasks that they proposed to execute in the most important period of adult life, suffers the condition of existential incompletism.

Evidence. It is worth emphasizing an apparently banal fact here: consciential maturity develops when an intraphysical consciousness switches from novelty magazines to science magazines.

Unfinished. The existential incompletist is one who left *unfinished* business in his or her human life.

Disinterest. This frequently occurs, because the social being, involved in material life, is not interested in knowing what one really came to do in human life. Thus, one only unconsciously or instinctively senses and identifies the undertakings or duties that he or she had proposed in the intermissive period.

EXISTENTIAL INCOMPLETION CAN CAUSE THE PREMATURE DEACTIVATION OF THE HUMAN BODY.

Existential anti-program. Existential anti-program attitudes can obviously provoke existential incompletism.

Causes. Erroneous thoughts are responsible for the majority of cases of existential incompletism that begins when intraphysical consciousnesses do not know how to ask the correct questions regarding his or her destiny, intraphysical life and existential program.

Mentalsoma. Erroneous thoughts constitute cases of thosenic or mentalsomatic para-pathology.

Nature. The nature of existential incompletism varies widely.

Extremes. Following are 3 examples of simple, but extreme, cases of incompletism. There is apparently no hope for these negligent or disorganized individuals:

1. **Dietitian.** The obese dietitian.
2. **Pulmonary specialist.** The pulmonary specialist who smokes.
3. **Psychiatrist.** The demented psychiatrist.

AN APPARENTLY SIMPLE FACTOR OF SELF-DISORGANIZATION CAN INDICATE AN UNNOTICED EXISTENTIAL INCOMPLETION *IN PROGRESS.*

Common. Unfortunately, the more obvious professional existential incompletists are the most common types of individuals. Take the following 3, for example:

A. **Businessperson.** The businessperson who becomes a drug trafficker.
B. **Driver.** A driver who becomes a highway assassin.
C. **Politician.** A politician who sinks to profiteering.

Money. They who live for money instead of living for ideas have a greater tendency to fall into existential incompletism.

Responsibility. Those intraphysical consciousnesses who have a great facility for writing, for example, have an enormous assistential responsibility towards others.

Assistance. Those who have good writing skills can help others more than the average person, through written communications that are capable of having a greater permanence in space and time.

Write. Those who write well and do not write anything for others who are semi-literate, inexperienced and less cultured, will often eventually find themselves with an incomplete existential program.

Test question. At this point, it is worth asking the following test question: "What have I done with the talents of my formal education?"

IF THE GREATEST TRIUMPH OF HUMAN CONSCIOUSNESS IS EXISTENTIAL COMPLETION, HIS OR HER GREATEST WEAKNESS, CLEARLY, IS EXISTENTIAL INCOMPLETION.

Intraphysical melancholy. The non-fulfillment of one's existential program generates the consciential state of intraphysical melancholy.

Crisis. The so-called *mid-life crisis in one's 40's* is a type of intraphysical melancholy that generally strikes intraphysical consciousnesses who senses his or her existential incompletion.

Extraphysical melancholy. Existential incompletion and *intra*physical melancholy generate *extra*physical melancholy, after the de-soma of the intraphysical consciousness.

Choices. Existential incompletion generates extraphysical melancholy, for example, when a consciousness discovers that he or she spent intraphysical life making inappropriate choices, victimizing him or herself with an ectopic existential program.

Para-pathology. The refined sensitivity of consciousness goes beyond the holochakra and the psychosoma. This can be illustrated by 3 facts, among others, that are observed in the para-pathology of the holosoma (see glossary):

A. **Para-scar.** When a consciousness commits a great loss-producing omission, a para-scar is produced in its consciential micro-universe.

B. **Fissure.** A veritable *fissure in the personality* is constituted by having an *energetic hole* (imbalance) in the holochakra.

C. **Mutilation.** Existential incompletion is equivalent to a temporary *mutilation of the mentalsoma*.

GENERALLY SPEAKING, MAKING A MISTAKE IS LIKE FROWNING: THEY BOTH TAKE MUCH MORE EFFORT AND ENERGY THAN DOING THINGS CORRECTLY OR SMILING.

Categories. In terms of its immediate effects, existential incompletism can be rationally classified into 2 categories:

1. **Personal.** When existential incompletion predisposes only one consciousness towards extraphysical melancholy (ego-karma).

2. **Groupal.** When existential completion predisposes an evolutionary group of consciousnesses towards extraphysical melancholy (group-karma).

Acracy. The word acracy, that comes from the Greek word signifying "absence of force" or "absence of self-control", is indicative of a weak will, one of the factors most responsible for innumerous failures (existential incompletion) in the execution of an existential program in this intraphysical dimension.

De-somatics. In de-somatics, we observe that *charismatic artists* are generally among the intraphysical consciousnesses, in human life, that are most pressured by the influence of the belly-brain, the cardio-chakra (heart chakra) and interconsciential intrusions. They are often elevated – through the instrument of modern mass communication – from poverty and material deprivation of all types, to the glitter of fame and fleeting *stardom*.

Existential Program Manual

Art. It is for this reason that many artists with the most noteworthy of talents, mega-star images and positions of leadership, who were predisposed to parapsychic mishaps or self-destructive tendencies (belly-brain), had their intraphysical lives abbreviated tragically and prematurely, leaving their mourning public behind (unthinking masses, existential robotization).

Casuistic. Following are 7 examples, selected from many, of artistic personalities who are intensely remembered and mourned over:

1. **James Dean,** icon of the youth in his era, 1931-1955, age 24.
2. **Isadora Duncan,** pioneer of modern dance, 1878-1927, age 49.
3. **Jimi Hendrix,** electric guitar genius, 1942-1970, age 28.
4. **John Lennon,** the first Beatle, 1940-1980, age 40.
5. **Marilyn Monroe,** Hollywood's mega-sex-symbol, 1926-1962, age 36.
6. **Elvis Presley,** a key figure in the international popular music revolution, 1935-1977, age 42.
7. **Rudolph Valentino,** the great lover of the silent screen, 1895-1926, age 31.

Athletes. Although in lesser quantity, athletes also de-soma (die) prematurely in tragic circumstances. For example: *Ayrton Senna,* the Formula 1 mega-champion, 1960-1994, age 34.

Politics. Still less in number, politicians also de-soma prematurely in tragic contexts. For example: *Martin Luther King,* the martyr of civil rights, 1929-1968, age 39.

Existential programology. In existential programology, the principal question to be answered in conscientiological research, in this context, is: Which of these personalities left human life in the condition of existential incompletists while – if it was the case – in the process of executing a consolation-task-oriented existential mini-program?

Evolutionology. An extraphysical evolutionologist is, doubtless, the consciousness best suited to answer this question regarding

34. EXISTENTIAL MULTI-COMPLETISM

Definition. *Existential multi-completism* is existential completion that is obtained through the execution of various existential programs in various consecutive intraphysical lives.

Synonymy. An equivalent expression for existential multi-completion: *extensive existential completism.*

Permanent-total-freedom-from-intrusion. After a consciousness attains the permanently-totally-intrusion-free condition, he or she tends to exhibit existential multi-completion, resulting in the multi-completist condition.

THE EXISTENTIAL MULTI-COMPLETIST IS A CONSCIOUSNESS WHO HAS SATISFACTORILY EXECUTED MORE THAN ONE EXISTENTIAL PROGRAM.

Self-relay. *Existential multi-completism* occurs when there is an assistential connection between the consciousness' existential programs, through consecutive self-relays, with at least the following 5 conditions:

A. **Life.** In more than 1 life.
B. **Somatics.** In more than 1 human body.
C. **Holochakrality.** In more than 1 energetic body.
D. **Chronology.** In more than 1 epoch.
E. **Intraphysicology.** In more than 1 intraphysical society.

Multi-completists. Existential multi-completists already exist, scattered throughout several sectors of social life on Earth, in certain areas of science, education, art and politics.

Questions. Do you, the reader, consider yourself a completist? Are you preparing yourself to be a multi-completist? Could you be a multi-completist? Do you know a multi-completist?

Self-organization. Self-organization, not rarely down to the smallest detail, is indispensable for the achievement of existential multi-completion.

Test question. If one wishes to find out if his or her personal organization is at a good level, they can answer the following test question: "Do the drawers of the cabinet under my bathroom sink have a written index that lists the drawer's contents?"

Behavior. It is rational to consider that behavior patterns which have remained unchanged over many centuries, in an intraphysical society or a traditional social holothosene will, in certain cases, also require *multi-existential recycling* through self-relays and continued existential multi-completions. This will allow a consciousness, by him or herself, to achieve the broader intraconsciential openness that we currently seek through conscientiology. Consider the following 5 examples of multi-secular behavior patterns:

1. **Alcoholism.**
2. **Bull fighting.**
3. **Monarchy.**
4. **Smoking.**
5. **Sumo wrestling.**

IN THE INTERMISSIVE COURSE, THE EXTRAPHYSICAL CONSCIOUSNESS STUDIES THE AUTOBIOGRAPHY OF HIS OR HER MOST RECENT EXISTENTIAL INCOMPLETION (OR COMPLETION).

35. EXISTENTIAL MORATORIUM

Definition. The *existential moratorium* is an extension added to complement one's human life, granted to the deserving human consciousness for fraternal efforts and performance.

Objective. The objective of the existential moratorium is to offer conditions that allow a consciousness to clear up omissions or seek to reasonably execute unfinished tasks.

Postponement. The existential moratorium represents a positive *postponement* of the deactivation *of the human body*.

Gaps. When an individual examines the directives of his or her existential program in greater detail, they might discover gaps or fundamental omissions in the *entire* framework of the tasks' execution. At this point, they may receive an existential moratorium.

Trophy. If existential completism is the diploma of human life, existential moratorium is the intraphysical consciousness' trophy.

Intraphysical euphoria. Intraphysical euphoria (generated by intraphysical completion) is the ideal condition that predisposes the acquisition of a positive existential moratorium.

EXISTENTIAL MORATORIUM PRESENTS 2 LOGICALLY DISTINCT CATEGORIES: EXISTENTIAL MINI-MORATORIUM AND MAXI-MORATORIUM.

36. EXISTENTIAL MINI-MORATORIUM

Definition. The existential moratorium can be deficiency-based – an *existential mini-moratorium* specific to existential incompletism.

Synonymy. Expressions equivalent to *existential mini-moratorium: deficient existential moratorium; restricted existential moratorium.*

Self-help. In the case of an existential mini-moratorium, the incompletist intraphysical consciousness is mostly being aided, as they receive a complementary period of human existence in order to complete (100%) what they had left undone.

Deficit. This denotes an opportunity to compensate for one's *holo-karmic deficit* (deficiency-base) or to achieve the condition of existential completism regarding one's existential program, the finishing of an incomplete intraphysical mandate.

Oversight. Incompletism, in this case, occurs through personal oversight or lack of an overall perception of one's own actions during the decades of human life.

IN OUR HUMAN ACTS, EITHER DISCERNMENT OR CARELESSNESS GENERALLY PREDOMINATES. WHICH QUALITY PREVAILS IN YOU?

37. EXISTENTIAL MAXI-MORATORIUM

Definition. Existential moratorium can be based on a greatly positive net balance – an existential maxi-program having a wholesale approach, specific to existential completism, or the concession of *honor due to the merit* of existential completism.

Synonymy. These 4 expressions are equivalent to *existential maxi-moratorium:*

A. *Honor due to existential merit.*
B. *Existential mega-moratorium.*
C. *Full existential moratorium.*
D. *Greatly positive net balance existential moratorium.*

Poly-karmality. The existential maxi-moratorium is a healthy *addition* in terms of the results of one's life program, in the practice of universalism and maxi-fraternity, and has a poly-karmic foundation.

Needs. Every intraphysical consciousness needs others, but an intraphysical-consciousness-leader needs many more, according to the talents of each one.

Hetero-help. In an existential maxi-moratorium, which is superior to an existential mini-moratorium in all senses, an intraphysical consciousness who is a *completist* helps more than he or she is helped.

Positive net balance. In an existential maxi-moratorium, an intraphysical consciousness receives a complementary period of human existence in order to expand upon what they have already accomplished well and completely *(holo-karmic positive net balance).*

Evolutionologist. In either of its 2 categories, an existential moratorium is the result of the direct, cosmoethic intercession of the evolutionologist or evolutionary orientor of the intraphysical consciousnesses' karmic group.

Recycling. Two or three existential moratoriums can occur, and can include the physiological recycling of the moratoriumist's soma.

Macro-somas. The physiological recycling of the soma is obviously more likely to occur with those having a macro-soma.

Groupal. There are very rare cases of groupal existential moratorium, within the evolutionary groupality of mini-cogs involved in the interconsciential and multi-dimensional assistential maxi-mechanism.

Future. It is hoped that, in the near future, groupal existential moratoriums become more common and include individuals with macro-somas.

Effort. In order to manifest these realities in intraphysical life, your existential program, completion and moratorium, it is important that you rely greatly on your personal efforts in the here-and-now.

Heroism. There is silent heroism behind every existential maxi-moratorium.

Neophobia. The existential maxi-moratorium increases the efficiency in the completion of one's task and can provoke *involuntary evolutionary rapes* (forced evolution) upon neophobic intraphysical consciousnesses who are in the peripheral evolutionary echelons (ranks) of this task.

THE COMPLEMENT OF TIME PROVIDED IN AN EXISTENTIAL MORATORIUM VARIES FROM DAYS TO MONTHS TO DECADES.

Binomial. The *binomial abnegation-existential-maxi-moratorium* is the most intelligent solution for the execution of any category of existential program. Strictly speaking, existential maxi-moratoriums do not exist without abnegation on the part of the intraphysical consciousness.

Trinomial. The *trinomial existential-program-completism-maxi-moratorium* is the beginning, middle and end of the abnegated intraphysical consciousness' entire concentrated effort (realization) in this Earth-school, in the role of outstanding student, *honor student,* conscious assistential mini-cog, or lucid consciential epicenter or completist – independent of the level of existential program.

THE LESS ILL, MORE EXPERIENCED INDIVIDUAL HELPS THOSE MORE ILL AND LESS EXPERIENCED BEINGS. THIS IS THE BASIC LAW OF INTERCONSCIENTIAL ASSISTANCE.

38. EVOLUTIONARY PRE-REQUISITES

Universe. The realities of the universe exist and act independent of our level of discernment or our depth of understanding about Humanity's relative leading-edge truths.

IGNORING A PROBLEM, AS SMALL AS IT MAY BE, DOES NOT BRING THE IGNORANT CONSCIOUSNESS INNER SECURITY.

Pre-requisites. For example, there are 11 fundamental pre-requisites that need to be conquered little-by-little by the individual, that allow him or her to achieve new evolutionary levels:

1. **Sub-humanity.** Being a sub-human is pre-requisite to becoming human.
2. **Pre-serenissimus.** Being a pre-serenissimus is pre-requisite to achieving the permanently-totally-intrusion-free condition.
3. **Permanently-totally-intrusion-free.** Being permanently-totally-intrusion-free is pre-requisite to becoming an evolutionologist.
4. **Evolutionology.** Being an evolutionologist is pre-requisite to becoming a serenissimus.
5. **Serenism.** Being a serenissimus is pre-requisite to becoming a free consciousness (FC – a consciousness who has reached the end of the rebirth cycle).
6. **Consolation.** Having performed the consolation task is pre-requisite to executing the clarification task.
7. **Retailing.** Having practiced consciential retailing is pre-requisite to performing consciential wholesaling.
8. **Group-karmality.** Having experienced group-karmality is pre-requisite to experiencing poly-karmality.

9. **Existential mini-program.** Having completed an existential mini-program is pre-requisite to receiving the task of an existential maxi-program.

10. **Existential completism.** Having achieved existential completism is pre-requisite to enjoying extraphysical euphoria.

11. **Macro-soma.** Having achieved existential completism is pre-requisite for receiving a macro-soma.

THE PRIORITIZATION OF CONSCIENTIAL CULTURE IS MUCH MORE IMPORTANT THAN MONEY OR TEMPORAL POWER FOR INTRAPHYSICAL CONSCIOUSNESSES.

39. MINIMUMS AND MAXIMUMS

Conditions. It is important for the interested researcher, at this point in his or her research, to consider the details that characterize the intra and extra-consciential evolutionary condition, in terms of the multiple possibilities for development and completion of the existential program.

Panoramic view. An instructive and exhaustive listing of minimal and maximal talents (mini and mega-*weak*-traits or mini and mega-*strong*-traits) has been provided in a panoramic manner for self-evaluation.

Mini-traits. Consciential mini-traits are characterized by 13 or more intra and extra-consciential conditions:

A. Initial condition.
B. Lesser (minor).
C. Elementary.
D. Simplistic.
E. Retailer.
F. Recipient.
G. Ego-karmic/group-karmic.
H. Dependency.
I. Factionalism.
J. Maxi-cog/mini-mechanism.
K. Quantitative.
L. Belly-brain (still a deficit).
M. Limited.

IT IS WORTH POINTING OUT THAT A CONSCIENTIAL MINI-TRAIT DOES NOT ALWAYS REPRESENT A WEAK TRAIT: **IT CAN BE A PRE-STRONG-TRAIT.**

Maxi-traits. Consciential maxi-traits are characterized by 13 or more intra and extra-consciential conditions:

A. Advanced condition.
B. Greater (major).
C. Superior.
D. Complex.
E. Wholesaler.
F. Donator.
G. Group-karmic/poly-karmic.
H. Self-sufficiency.
I. Maxi-fraternity.
J. Mini-cog/maxi-mechanism.
K. Qualitative.
L. Mentalsomatic (already a great positive net balance).
M. Full.

CONSCIENTIAL DE-REPRESSION BEGINS IN THE SOMA AND, THROUGH SELF-ORGANIZATION, PROCEEDS UNTIL IT REACHES THE MENTALSOMA.

Mini-conquests. Following are 10 personal conquests within the scope of mini-trait manifestations:

A. **Existential mini-program:** consolation task, retailing, group-karmality.
B. **Mini-soma:** somaticity, common soma.
C. **Mini-endowment:** consciential mono-endowment.
D. **Mini-conscientiality:** consciential retailing.
E. **Mini-communication:** mediumship, channeling.
F. **Mini-task:** consolation task.
G. **Mini-dissidence:** personal limitation, neophobia.
H. **Existential mini-completion:** existential mini-program, consolation task.
I. **Existential mini-moratorium:** ego-karmality.
J. **Mini-evolution:** merely pre-serenissimus.

Maxi-conquests. Following are 10 personal conquests within the scope of maxi-trait manifestations:

A. **Existential maxi-program:** clarification task, wholesaling, poly-karmality.
B. **Maxi-soma:** somaticity, macro-soma.
C. **Maxi-endowment:** consciential tri-endowment (or more).
D. **Maxi-conscientiality:** consciential wholesaling.
E. **Maxi-communication:** lucid projectability.
F. **Maxi-task:** clarification task.
G. **Maxi-dissidence:** personal renovation, neophilia.
H. **Existential maxi-completism:** existential maxi-program, clarification task.
I. **Existential maxi-moratorium:** poly-karmality.
J. **Maxi-evolution:** permanently-totally-intrusion-free (or beyond this, in the future).

PARA-GENETICS IS THE ACCUMULATION OF SCARS – CLOSED WOUNDS – ON THE MENTALSOMA OF THE EXTRAPHYSICAL CONSCIOUSNESS WHO IS REBORN ON EARTH.

40. Permanent-total-freedom-from-intrusion

Definition. *Permanent-total-freedom-from-intrusion* is the evolutionary consciential quality of the individual who is permanently-totally-intrusion-free and completely aware of this condition with regards to assistential tasks rendered towards other consciousnesses.

Achievement of the permanent-total-intrusion-free condition during one's life is generally indispensable for the execution of the more advanced existential maxi-programs.

Evolution. The permanently-totally-intrusion-free condition is the next evolutionary step for the pre-serenissimus intraphysical consciousness, whether he or she is an existential recycler, existential invertor, penta practitioner or consciential epicenter.

***Strong* traits.** Following are 7 strong traits characteristic of the female or male permanently-totally-intrusion-free being:

1. **VS.** Installs a high quality vibrational state, or preventative VS when and where he or she wishes, sensing and discriminating his or her consciential energies.

2. **Self-defense.** Maintains an uninterrupted condition of energetic self-defense in his or her consciential micro-universe, through the experience of energetic, intra-consciential and parapsychic signals. Thus, the individual will be able to detect the presence of healthy and ill consciousnesses where he or she lives and wherever he or she goes, harmonizing what he or she can everywhere.

3. **Liberation.** No longer suffers unconscious interconsciential mini-intrusions, although living at the front-line of interpersonal human experiences.

4. **Self-cure.** Effects the self-cure of mini-illnesses or small inconveniences related to the human being.

5. **Consciential epicenter.** Has an obvious energetic presence where they go, as a consciential epicenter.

6. **Penta.** Practices penta daily.

7. **Assistentiality.** Cooperates lucidly, without trauma, in the role of intra and extraphysical assistential bait, in favor of other consciousnesses.

THE GREATEST ACHIEVEMENT THAT CAN BE REALIZED BY THE EXECUTOR OF AN EXISTENTIAL PROGRAM IS TO TRANSCEND THE FORCES THAT SHAPE HIS OR HER INTRAPHYSICAL LIFE.

GLOSSARY OF CONSCIENTIOLOGY

Advanced existential program – *Existential program* of an *intraphysical consciousness* who is an evolutionary leader, performing within a specific libertarian *group-karmic* task that is more universalist and poly-karmic in nature. This individual serves as a lucid, *mini*-cog acting within a *maxi*-mechanism of a multi-dimensional team.

Alternate intraphysical pre-serenissimus – *Intraphysical consciousness* capable of simultaneously living consciously in the waking state as well as projected in the extraphysical dimensions, from time-to-time.

Andro-chakra (*andro* + *chakra*) – A man's *sex-chakra*.

Andro-thosene (neologism: *andro* + *tho* + *sen* + *ene*) – *Thosene* of the primitive masculine or *macho* man.

Animism (Latin: *animus,* soul) – Set of *intra* and *extracorporeal* phenomena produced by the *intraphysical consciousness* without external interference. Example: the phenomenon of *conscious projection* induced by one's own will.

Anti-thosene (*anti* + *tho* + *sen* + *ene*) – Antagonistic *thosene*, common in refutations, omni-questionings and in productive debates.

Assisted conscious projection – Projection wherein a *consciousness* finds him or herself directly assisted during the experience by a *Helper* who is almost always an expert in lucid *projectability*.

Auric coupling – Interfusion of *holochakral* energies between 2 or more *consciousnesses*.

Behavior-pattern – *Typical pattern of behavior.*

Behavior-exception – *Atypical, ectopic or dislocated pattern of behavior.*

Belly-brain – Abdominal sub-brain; the *umbilical-chakra* (center of *consciential energy* located above the navel), when unconsciously selected by an *intraphysical consciousness*, who is still at a vulgar stage of evolution, for the task of basing his or her manifestations upon. The *belly-brain, abdominal brain, abdomi-*

nal pseudo-brain, or *abdominal sub-brain*, is a *parody* of the natural, encephalic brain (*coronal-chakra* and *frontal-chakra*); an indefensible embarrassment in conscious self-evolution.

Biothosene (*bio* + *tho* + *sen* + *ene*) – *Thosene* specifically related to *human consciousness*.

Brady-thosene (*brady* + *tho* + *sen* + *ene*) – *Thosene* having a sluggish flow, pertaining to the slow-minded *human consciousness*.

Cardio-chakra (*cardio* + *chakra*) – The fourth basic chakra; influential agent in the emotionality of an *intraphysical consciousness*; vitalizes the heart and lungs; heart chakra.

Chakra – A nucleus or defined field of *consciential energy*. The totality of the many chakras in one's energetic system constitutes the *holochakra* or *energetic para-body*. The *holochakra*, inside the *soma*, forms a junction between the *soma* and *psychosoma*, acting as a point of connection through which *consciential energy* flows from one *vehicle* to another.

Chirosoma (*chiro* + *soma*) – The body considered specifically in regards to the use of hands or manual work.

Clarification task – Advanced personal or group task of enlightenment or clarification.

Con – Hypothetical unit of measure of the lucidity of an *intraphysical* or *extraphysical consciousness*.

Conscientese – Telepathic non-symbolic idiom that is native to the *consciential dimensions* of very evolved *extraphysical* societies.

Consciential amentia – Condition in which a *consciousness* is incapable of thinking with reasonable mental balance.

Consciential basement – Phase of infantile and adolescent manifestations of *intraphysical consciousness* up until adulthood, characterized by a predominance of the more primitive weak traits of *consciousness* – *consciousness* being multi-vehicular, multi-existential and multi-millenary.

Consciential concentration – The direct, unswerving, focusing of one's senses, *consciential* attributes, will and intention upon a singular object.

Consciential continuism – Condition of continuity of *consciential* life through preview and evolutionary self-relay, or rather: the incessant correction of one's experience of the present moment, those immediately anterior and posterior, in a cohesive and unified whole, without loss of continuity or impervious *consciential* experiences; condition of being lucid from lifetime to lifetime, including when your body is asleep, etc.

Consciential dermatological (superficial) **approaches** – Compound expression attributed to the conventional, physicalist sciences that are subordinated to the newtonian-cartesian, mechanistic paradigm, and focus their research only on the soma – not availing themselves to the instrumentation necessary for the direct, technical investigation of *consciousness* itself; dermatological approaches of *intraphysical consciousness*. *Peri-consciential* sciences.

Consciential ectopia – Unsatisfactory execution of one's *existential program* in an eccentric, dislocated manner, outside the programming chosen for the individual's *intraphysical life*.

Consciential energy – *Immanent energy* that a *consciousness* employs in its general manifestations; the *ene* of *thosene*; personal energy.

Consciential epicenter – Key *intraphysical consciousness* who becomes a fulcrum of interdimensional lucidity, assistentiality and constructiveness through the use of the *extraphysical clinic*. Directly related to *penta* or personal energetic task.

Consciential era – That era in which the average *intraphysical consciousness* finds him or herself sufficiently evolved, through impacts, personal redefinition and revolutions created through experiences of *lucid projectability*, to implant the *priority of self-conscientiality*.

Consciential eunuch – Individual *conscientially* castrated and manipulated by the sectarian domesticators of *satisfied human automatons (robots)*, who are modern slaves of the unthinking masses.

Consciential gestation – Evolutionary productivity on the part of an *intraphysical consciousness* in terms of the execution of its *existential program*.

Consciential hyperspace – *Extraphysical consciential* dimensions.

Consciential micro-universe – *Consciousness* when considered as a whole, including all of its attributes, *thosenes* and manifestations in its evolution. The micro-cosmos of *consciousness* in relation to the macro-cosmos of the universe.

Consciential mono-capability – *Intraphysical life* under the pressure of constant *intrusions* by ill beings. This is experienced by vulgar *intraphysical consciousnesses* having few talents and no versatility.

Consciential para-comatose – State of *extraphysical* coma of a *projected intraphysical consciousness*, who invariably remains unconscious and, therefore, has no recall of *extraphysical* events.

Consciential paradigm – Leading-theory of *Conscientiology*, founded in *consciousness* itself.

Consciential restriction – Restriction of consciousness due to the process of manifestation in the physical state, in which one's natural level of awareness is reduced.

Consciential retailing – A rudimentary system of individual behavior characterized by lesser, isolated *consciential* actions having a minimum of productive results or important evolutionary effects.

Consciential scaffolds – Dispensable psychological or physical *crutches* used by *consciousness*.

Consciential self-bilocation (Latin: *bis*, two; and *locus*, place) – Act whereby an *intraphysical projector* encounters and contemplates his or her own human body (*soma*) face-to-face, when his or her *consciousness* is outside of the *soma* (in the case of an *intraphysical consciousness*) and in another vehicle of *consciential* manifestation.

Consciential tri-capability – Quality of the 3 talents most useful to *conscientiology* – intellectuality, psychic abilities and communicability – when found together.

Consciential wholesaling – Behavior of an individual characterized by a tendency to approach issues in a comprehensive or wholesale manner so as not to leave negative evolutionary loose ends or *gaps* behind.

Conscientiocentric institution – That institution which centralizes its objectives on *consciousness* and its evolution, as is the case with the International Institute of Projectiology (IIP); *consciential* cooperative, in *Conscientiological* Society, having employment and *consciential* ties at its foundation.

Conscientiogram – Technical plan for evaluative measurement of the evolutionary level of *consciousness*; *consciential mega-test* having *Homo sapiens serenissimus* as a model – *Serenissimus* being responsible for a positive *ego-karmic account*. The *conscientiogram* is the basic instrument employed in *conscientiometric* tests.

Conscientiologist – *Intraphysical consciousness* engaged in the continuing study and objective experimentation in the field of *conscientiology* research. The *conscientiologist* operates as an agent of evolutionary renovation (*retrocognitive agent*), in the liberating work of *consciousnesses* in general.

Conscientiology – Science that studies *consciousness* in an integral, *holosomatic*, multi-dimensional multi-millenary, multi-existential manner and, overall, according to its reactions with regards to immanent energy, *consciential energy* and its own multiple states of being.

Conscientiometry – Discipline that studies *consciential* measurements through the use of resources and methods offered by *Conscientiology*, capable of establishing the possible bases of the *mathematical analysis of consciousness*. The *conscientiogram* is the principle instrument used in *conscientiometry*.

Conscientiotherapy – Treatment, alleviation or remission of disturbances of *consciousness* executed through the resources and techniques derived from *Conscientiology*.

Conscious projection (CP) – Projection of *an intraphysical consciousness* beyond the soma; extracorporeal experience; out-of-body experience (OBE).

Consolation task – An elementary-level personal or group *assistential task of consolation*.

Coronal-chakra (*coronal* + *chakra*) – Chakra at the top of the head, crowning the *holochakra*; crown chakra.

Cosmo-consciousness – Condition of a *consciousness'* inner awareness of the cosmos, of life and the order of the universe, in an intellectual and *cosmoethical* exaltation that is impossible to describe. In this case, a *consciousness* senses the living presence of the universe around him or her, in an indivisible unity. *Interconsciential* communication occurs in this peculiar condition.

Cosmoethic (*cosmo + ethic*) – Ethic or reflection over the cosmic, multi-dimensional morality that defines *holomaturity*. *Cosmoethic* is situated beyond the social, intraphysical morality, or that which presents itself to be beyond any human label.

Cosmoethical mimicry – Productive social impulse towards imitation of one's evolved forebears.

Cosmoethicality – A *consciousness'* *cosmoethic* nature.

Cosmothosene (*cosmo + tho + sen + ene*) – *Thosene* specifically related to *conscientese* or the state of *cosmoconsciousness*; form of communication of *conscientese*.

Co-thosene (*co + tho + sen + ene*) – *Thosene* specifically related to the collective actions of a chorus, of those praying in groups or crowds.

Counter-body – Same as *holochakra*, the vehicle of an *intraphysical consciousness'* *consciential energy;* energetic body.

Counter-thosene (*counter + tho + sen + ene*) – Intraconsciential *thosene* of an *intraphysical consciousness*; mute mental refutation; mental word; mute thosene; a type of *intra-thosene*.

Daydream – Fanciful story created by one's imagination during the waking state of *human consciousness*.

De-soma (*de + soma*) – Somatic deactivation, impending and inevitable for all *intraphysical consciousnesses*; final projection; *first death*; biological death; monothanatosis. De-soma (by itself) or *first de-soma* is the deactivation of the human body or *soma* (biological death). Second *de-soma* is the deactivation of the *holochakra*. Third *de-soma* is the deactivation of the *psychosoma*.

Destructive macro-PK – Harmful PK (*psychokinesis*) capable of causing losses to the *intraphysical consciousness*. Destructive macro-PK can prove fatal.

Domiciliary holo-thosene – Physical base; bedroom that has been energetically shielded; *extraphysical clinic*.

Dream – Natural *consciential* state that is intermediary between the waking state and natural sleep. Dreams are characterized by a set of ideas and images that present themselves to *consciousness*. An afflictive dream includes agitation, anguish and oppression in its development, and is known as: *nightmare*; *night terror*; *nightmarish hallucination*.

Ego-karma (*ego* + *karma*) – Principle of cause and effect acting in the evolution of *consciousness*, when centered exclusively around the ego per se. State wherein one's free will is restricted by infantile egocentrism.

Egothosene (*ego* + *tho* + *sen* + *ene*) – Same as *self-thosene*; *unit of measurement* of *consciential* egotism according to *Conscientiology* or, more appropriately, according to *Conscientiometry*.

Energetic dimension – Energetic dimension of *consciousnesses*; *holochakral* dimension; *third-and-a-half* dimension. Dimension natural to the *holochakra*.

Energetic intrusion – Invasion of an *intraphysical consciousness* by another using *consciential energies* or *holo-chakra*; *holo-chakral intrusion*.

Energetic maxi-spring – Condition of a maximized or prolonged *energetic spring* (energetic plenitude).

Energetic mini-spring – Condition of a minimal or ephemeral *energetic spring* (energetic plenitude).

Energetic spring – A more-or-less long-lasting condition wherein one's *consciential energies* exhibit an optimal, healthy, constructive profile.

Energetic spring by two – *Energetic spring* of an *evolutionary duo*, the partners of which truly love each other and have mastered the application of healthy consciential energy with complete lucidity, building their *existential program* through *consciential gestations*.

Enumerology – Didactic technique of processing texts based on informative self-critiquing.

Evolutionary duo – Two *consciousnesses* that interact positively in joint evolution; existential condition of *cooperative evolutionality* by two individuals.

Evolutionary orientor – *Consciousness* who is assistential in the intelligent coordination of an individual's *existential program*, or in the *consciential* evolution of one or more individuals in the same karmic group; *Helper;* Evolutionary condition inbetween *Serenissimus* and the status of being *completely and permanently without intrusion.*

Existential completism – Condition of a *human consciousness' existential program* having been completed.

Existential inversion – Technique of optimizing one's *consciential* performance in the *preparatory phase* of the individual's *existential program* (up through 35 years of physical age).

Existential invertability – Quality of *intraphysical execution* of *existential inversion.*

Existential invertor – One who disposes him or herself to the execution of *existential inversion* in *intraphysical life.*

Existential maxi-moratorium – Condition of a greater *existential moratorium* or that which occurs for a *completist*, coming as an addition to his or her finished *existential program*; execution of a *healthy extension* to an *existential mandate* that has been concluded.

Existential maxi-program – *Maximal existential program* having a wholesale approach. It targets the execution of tasks of universalism and *maxi-fraternity* having *poly-karmic* bases.

Existential mini-moratorium – Condition of a lesser *existential moratorium* or that which occurs for an , coming as an opportunity to compensate for his or her holo-karmic *deficit* or to achieve the status of *completist regarding* his or her *existential program*; the finishing of a still incomplete *existential mandate.*

Existential mini-program – *Existential program* targeting the execution of a minimal, *group-karmic task.*

Existential moratorium – An extension of *intraphysical life* given to selected *intraphysical consciousnesses* according to their *holo-karmic merit.* An *existential moratorium* can be based on deficiency in (*existential mini-moratorium*) or completion of (*existential maxi-moratorium*) the individual's *existential program*.

Existential moratoriumist – One who receives an existential moratorium; moratoriumist.

Existential program – Specific program of each *intraphysical consciousness*, to be executed in their current *intraphysical life*.

Existential recyclability – Quality of the *intraphysical* execution of *existential recycling*.

Existential programology – The formal study of the existential program; a branch of conscientiology.

Existential recycler – *Intraphysical consciousness* who disposes him or herself to the execution of *existential recycling*.

Existential recycling – Technique for the realization of one's *existential program*, executed by a *human consciousness*.

Existential robotization – Condition of a tropospheric *intraphysical consciousness* who is enslaved to *intraphysicality* or quadridimensionality.

Existential self-mimicry – Imitation of one's own past experiences, be they related to their *intraphysical* life or to previous *intraphysical* lives.

Existential seriation – 1. Evolutionary *existential seriation* of *consciousness*; successive existences; *intraphysical* rebirths in series. 2. *Intraphysical* or human life. Outworn synonym: *reincarnation*; this archaic word no longer serves those more serious individuals dedicated to leading-edge *consciousness* research.

Extraphysical – Relative to what is outside, or beyond, the *intraphysical* or human state; *consciential* state *less physical* than the human body; non-physical.

Extraphysical agenda – written notes of priority *consciential extraphysical* targets – beings, locales or ideas – that the projected individual seeks to gradually reach, in a chronological manner, establishing intelligent plans for his or her development.

Extraphysical approach – Contact of a *consciousness* with another in the *extraphysical* dimensions.

Extraphysical catatonia – Fixed condition whereby a projected *intraphysical consciousness* performs stereotypical repetitive acts that are generally useless or dispensable in terms of his or her evolution.

Extraphysical clinic – *Extraphysical* treatment center of an *intraphysical epicenter* (*penta* practitioner); *extraphysical clinic*. The resources and *extraphysical installations* of the *extraphysical clinic* are numerous and remarkable. The *extraphysical clinic* is a domiciliary *holothosene*.

Extraphysical community – A common lifestyle setting of *extraphysical consciousnesses* in an *extraphysical* dimension.

Extraphysical Consciousness – *Para-citizen* of *extraphysical society*; disembodied *consciousness*. Outworn synonym: *discarnate*.

Extraphysical euphoria – Euphoria experienced after biological death due to the reasonably satisfactory completion of one's *existential program; post-mortem* euphoria; *para-euphoria*; *post-somatic euphoria*.

Extraphysical melancholy – Condition of *extraphysical, post-somatic or post-mortem melancholy; para-melancholy*.

Extraphysical monitoring – Condition wherein assistance is given by healthy *extraphysical consciousnesses* to a balanced *intraphysical consciousness*, when said individual is performing balanced tasks of consolation or clarification.

Extraphysical precognition (Latin: *pre*, before; *cognoscere*, know) – Perceptive faculty whereby a *consciousness*, while fully projected outside the human body, comes to know about indeterminate upcoming facts, as well as objects, scenes and distant forms, in the future.

Extraphysical romance – Totality of acts whereby an *intraphysical consciousness* maintains a healthy or positive romantic relationship while projected outside the body.

Extraphysical society – Society of *extraphysical consciousnesses*.

Free consciousness (Latin: *con* + *scientia*, with knowing) – *Extraphysical consciousness* who has definitively liberated him or herself *(deactivation)* from the *psychosoma* or emotional body and the web of existential seriation *(rebirth cycle)*. *Free consciousness* is situated in the *evolutionary hierarchy* above *Homo sapiens serenissimus*.

Geo-energy (*geo* + *energy*) – *Immanent energy* deriving from the soil or earth and absorbed by an *intraphysical consciousness* through the *pre-kundalini* (sole) chakras. Archaic expression: *telluric energy*.

Golden cord – Supposed energetic element – similar to a remote control – that maintains the *mentalsoma* connected to the *extraphysical* brain of the *psychosoma*.

Grapho-thosene (*grapho* + *tho* + *sen* + *ene*) – The *thosenic signature* of a *human consciousness*.

Group of existential inverters – *Intraphysical consciousnesses* meeting together in groups, objectifying experimentation in planned *existential inversion*.

Group of existential recyclers – *Intraphysical consciousnesses* meeting together in groups, objectifying experimentation in planned existential recycling.

Groupality – Quality of the *evolutionary group* of a *consciousness;* condition of *group evolutionality*.

Group-karma (*group* + *karma*) – Principle of cause and effect acting in the evolution of *consciousness*, when pertaining to the *evolutionary group*. State wherein one's free will is bound to one's *evolutionary group*.

Group-karmic course – Sum total of stages (intraphysical lives) of *consciousness* wherein one is more closely tied to one's *consciential evolutionary group*.

Group-karmic inter-prison – Condition of *group-karmic* inseparability from an evolutionary *consciential* principle or from a specific *consciousness*.

Group-thosene – A sectarian, corporate, *anti-poly-karmic thosene*. A *group-thosene* can also be constructive.

Gyno-chakra (*gyno* + *chakra*) – *Sex-chakra* of a woman.

Gyno-soma (*gyno* + *soma*) – The female human body, specialized in the animal reproduction of *intraphysical consciousness* in *intraphysical life;* aphrodisiac body.

Gyno-thosene (*gyno* + *tho* + *sen* + *ene*) – *Thosene* specifically related to feminine language and communicability.

Hallucination (Latin: *hallucinari*, to err) – Apparent perception of an external object that is not present in the moment; mental error in one's sensory perceptions which are not founded in objective reality.

Helper – *Extraphysical consciousness* that assists or serves as an auxiliary to one or more *intraphysical consciousnesses*; *extraphysical* benefactor. Outworn equivalent expressions: *guardian angel; angel of light; angel; mentor; spirit guide.*

Hetero-thosene (*hetero* + *tho* + *sen* + *ene*) – The *thosene* of another in relation to ourself.

Holo-archive – Compilation of information from artifacts of knowledge.

Holo-chakra (*holo* + *chakra*) – *Extraphysical energetic body* of *human consciousness*. Sum total of all chakras in one's energetic system; energetic double; energetic body; pranic body.

Holochakral existence – *Intraphysical life* or the existential seriation of the *intraphysical existences* of *human consciousness*.

Holochakral intrusion – Invasion of an *intraphysical consciousness* by another using the *holo-chakra* or *consciential energies; energetic intrusion.*

Holochakral looseness – Condition of relative freedom of action of the *energetic para-body* of an *intraphysical consciousness,* as compared to its *psychosoma* and *soma.*

Holochakral seduction – Energetic action of one *consciousness* over another (or others) with a more-or-less conscious intention of domination.

Holo-chakrality – Qualities of the manifestations of *intraphysical consciousness* deriving from the *holochakra.*

Holo-karma (*holo* + *karma*) – The 3 types of *consciential* actions and reactions – *ego-karma, group-karma* and *poly-karma* – within the acting principles of cause and effect in evolution of *consciousness. Ego-karma, group-karma* and *poly-karma* when considered as a whole.

Holomaturity (*holo* + *maturity*) – Condition of the integrated maturity – biological, psychological, *holosomatic* and multi-dimensional – of *human consciousness.*

Holomemory (*holo* + *memory*) – Causal, compound, multi-millenary, multi-existential, implacable, uninterrupted, personal memory that retains all facts relative to *consciousness*; multi-memory; poly-memory.

Holo-orgasm (*holo* + *orgasm*) – *Holosomatic* orgasm; maximum ecstasy generated through the energy of the entire *holosoma*.

Holosoma *(holo + soma)* – Set of vehicles of manifestation of *intraphysical consciousness*: *soma, holochakra, psychosoma* and *mentalsoma;* set of vehicles of manifestation of *extraphysical consciousness: psychosoma* and *mentalsoma*.

Holosomatic homeostasis – Integrated, healthy state of harmony of the *holosoma.*

Holosomatic interfusion – State of maximal *sympathetic assimilation* between 2 *consciousnesses.*

Holosomatic intrusion – Invasion of an *intraphysical consciousness* by another using the entire *holosoma.*

Holosomatics – Discipline that studies the *holosoma.*

Holo-thosene (*holo* + *tho* + *sen* + *ene*) – Aggregated or consolidated *thosenes.* This word generates resistance in a wide band of serious readers of the sciences.

Homo sapiens serenissimus – A *consciousness* that is integrally experiencing its condition of lucid serenism; a *consciousness* that is about to pass through the third de-soma (end of rebirth cycle). Popular synonym: *Serenissimus.*

Hyper-acuity – The quality of maximum lucidity of an *intraphysical consciousness,* achieved through recuperation – as far as possible – of his or her cons.

Hyper-thosene (*hyper* + *tho* + *sen* + *ene*) – Heuristic *thosene;* original idea of a discovery; neophilic *thosene*; unit of measurement of invention, according to *Conscientiology.*

Hypnagogy (Greek: *hipnos*, sleep; and *agogos*, conductor) – Transitional twilight condition of *consciousness* between the waking state and natural sleep state. It is an altered state of *consciousness.*

Hypnopompy (Greek: *hipnos*, sleep; and *pompikós*, procession) – A transitional condition of natural sleep, prior to physical awakening. It is a semi-asleep state that precedes the act of waking up. It is characterized by dream images having auditory effects and hallucinatory visions that continue even after waking. It is an altered state of *consciousness*.

Hypo-thosene (*hypo* + *tho* + *sen* + *ene*) – Same as *proto-thosene* or *Phyto-thosene*.

Immanent energy – Primary energy, totally impersonal, neutral and dispersed in all objects or physical creations throughout the universe. It is an omnipotent form, and has still not been mastered by human *consciousness*. It is too subtle to be detected by existing instruments.

Incomplete couple – Couple composed of a man and woman who do not form an intimate couple (a couple that has complete sexual interactions), but who, nevertheless, maintain strong affectionate ties.

Incompletism – Condition wherein a *human consciousness' existential program* is incomplete.

Integrated maturity – State of a more evolved *consciential* maturity beyond biological (physical) or mental (psychological) maturity; *holomaturity*.

Interassistential – Of or pertaining to mutual assistance.

Interassistentiality – The evolutionary necessity for *human consciousnesses* to assist each other through logical, just and mature *interassistential works*.

Interconsciential climate – Condition of multiple understanding in an *interconsciential* encounter, established through *thosenes* having affinity, especially those *charged* with *consciential energy*. *Interconsciential climates* can vary greatly in intensity.

Interconsciential intrusion – Action exercised by a consciousness on another.

Interdimensionality – *Interconsciential* communication between many *intraphysical* (physical) and *extraphysical* (non-physical) *dimensions*.

Intermissibility – Quality of the period of intermission between two *intraphysical* lives of a *consciousness*.

Intermission – The *extraphysical* period between 2 of a *consciousness' existential seriations* (*rebirth cycle*).

Intermissive course – Sum total of disciplines and theoretical and practical experiences administered to an *extraphysical consciousness* during its period of *consciential intermission* between two *intraphysical* lives. This course occurs when one has achieved a determinate evolutionary level in one's cycle of personal existences. It has the aim of allowing *consciential completism* in the next *intraphysical life*.

Inter-personal apparition – Appearance of the *consciousness* of a *projector* before *intraphysical consciousnesses*.

Intra-conscientiality – Quality of the specific intimate manifestations of *consciousness*.

Intraphysical consciousness – Human personality; citizen of *intraphysical* society. Outworn synonym: *incarnate*.

Intraphysical euphoria – Euphoria experienced before *somatic* deactivation that is generated through the reasonably satisfactory completion of one's *existential program*; *pre-mortem* euphoria. Ideal condition predisposing one to have a positive *existential moratorium*.

Intraphysical melancholy – Condition of *intraphysical* or *pre-mortem melancholy*.

Intraphysical recycling – An *intraconsciential, existential, intraphysical recycling* or the cerebral renovation of an *intraphysical consciousness* through the creation of new synapses (interneural connections) capable of permitting the adjustment of one's *existential program*, the execution of *existential recycling*, *existential inversion*, the acquisition of new ideas, *neo-thosenes, hypo-thosenes* and other neophilic conquests of the self-motivated *human consciousness*.

Intraphysical societal virus – Any social *weak* trait in the *intraphysical life* of a *human consciousness*.

Intraphysical society – Society of *intraphysical consciousnesses*; human society.

Intraphysicality – Condition of *intraphysical* or human life, or of the existence of *human consciousness*.

Intra-thosene (*intra + tho + sen + ene*) – *Intraconsciential thosene* of *human consciousness*.

Existential Program Manual 155

Intrudability – Pathological, *interconsciential thosenic intrusion*. Out-dated equivalent expression: *obsession*. Numerous *intraphysical consciousnesses* are defensive regarding the use of this word.

Intrusive stigma – An evolutionary failure or derailing that is always dramatic and generally pathological, usually stemming from *consciential* self-obsession. This process generates either *intraphysical* or *extraphysical melancholy* and often results in psychic accidents.

Locked existence – Human experience or existential seriation without the production of *conscious projections* (CPs); tropospheric human life having only unconscious, vegetative projections characteristic of the state of evolutionary *extraphysical* coma; locked existential seriation.

Lucid projectability – Lucid, projective paraphysiological quality of *consciousness* capable of provoking the non-alignment of its *holosoma,* through the use of the will, as well as by other means.

Lucidity-recall (a binomial) – Set of two conditions indispensable to the *intraphysical consciousness* for the achievement of a fully satisfactory *lucid projection* outside the body.

Macro-soma (*macro + soma*) – Soma that is *super-customized* for the execution of a specific *existential program.*

Maxi-fraternity – Most evolved, universalist, interconsciential condition that is based on pure fraternity on the part of a *consciousness* who pardons others for transgressions but not him or herself; mega-brotherhood. *Maxi-fraternity* is an inevitable goal in the evolution of all *consciousnesses.*

Maxi-thosene (*maxi + tho + sen + ene*) – *Thosene* peculiar to *Free Consciousnesses.*

Mega-goal – A greater evolutionary objective for a *consciousness.*

Mega-power – The evolved condition of *cosmoethical*, magnum *consciential* lucidity.

Mega-strong trait – The maximal strong trait of a *consciousness.*

Mega-thosene (*mega + tho + sen + ene*) – Same as *ortho-thosene*.

Mega-weak trait – The maximal weak trait of a *consciousness*.

Mental projective target – Predetermined goal that an *intraphysical consciousness* endeavors to reach using will, intention, mentalization and decision upon noting him or herself lucid while outside the body.

Mentalsoma (*mental + soma*) – Mental body; extraphysical body of discernment of *consciousness*. Plural: *mentalsomas*.

Mentalsomatic cycle – The evolutionary cycle or course that a *consciousness* initiates in its condition of *free consciousness* upon the definitive deactivation of the *psychosoma* (*third death*), consequently living only with the *mentalsoma*.

Mentalsomaticity – Qualities of the manifestations of *intraphysical consciousness* deriving from the *mentalsoma*.

Metasoma (*meta + soma*) – Same as *psychosoma*, the extraphysical instrument of *extraphysical* and *intraphysical consciousnesses*.

Mini-thosene (*mini + tho + sen + ene*) – *Thosene* of a child, sometimes as a function of their still developing brain.

Mnemonic intrusion – Collision of the intrusive memory of an *extraphysical consciousness* upon the cerebral memory of an *intraphysical consciousness* who has been intruded upon (*para-amnesia*).

Mono-thanatose – Same as *de-soma*; *first death*.

Mono-thosene (*mono + tho + sen + ene*) – Repetitive *thosene*; fixed idea; mental echo; *re-thosene*.

Moratoriumist – existential moratoriumist.

Morpho-thosene (*morpho + tho + sen + ene*) – A thought or a group of thoughts when gathered together and expressed as having some type of *form*. Archaic expression now fallen out of use: *thought-form*. An accumulation of *morphothosenes* composes a *holothosene*.

Multi-dimensional self-awareness – Condition of lucid maturity of an *intraphysical consciousness* in terms of living a *multi-dimensionally* evolved *consciential* life. This condition is achieved through *lucid projectability*.

Multi-existential cycle – System or condition of continuous alternation – at our current, average evolutionary level – of an *intraphysical* rebirth period (*intraphysical* lifetime or *existential seriation*) followed by an *extraphysical somatic* post-deactivation period or *intermission* (*extraphysical* "lifetime").

Near-Death Experience (NDE) – Involuntary or forced *projection* due to critical circumstances pertaining to a *human consciousness*. NDE is common in cases of terminal illness and survivors of clinical death.

Neophilia – *Intraphysical consciousness'* easy adaptation to new situations, things and occurrences. Opposite of neophobia.

Neo-thosene (*neo + tho + sen + ene*) – *Thosene* of an *intraphysical consciousness* when operating with new synapses or interneural connections – a situation capable of provoking *intraconsciential recycling*; *unit of measurement* of *consciential* renovation, according to *Conscientiology* or, more appropriately, *Conscientiometry*.

Oneiro-thosene – (*oneiro + tho + sen + ene*) – Dream thosene. Same as *patho-thosene*.

Orgasmic aura (Latin: *aura*, wisp of air)   Holochakral energy of *facies sexualis* of a man or woman at the exact moment of sexual orgasm or climax.

Ortho-thosene (*ortho + tho + sen + ene*) – A *just* or *cosmoethical thosene*, pertaining to *consciential holomaturity*; a *unit of measurement* of practical *cosmoethics*, according to *Conscientiometry*.

Pangraphy – Broad, sophisticated multi-modal psychic writing.

Para – Prefix that signifies *beyond* or *beside*, as in *parabrain*. Also signifies *extraphysical*.

Para-brain – *Extraphysical* brain of the *psychosoma* of a *consciousness* in the *extraphysical* (*extraphysical consciousness*), *intraphysical* (*intraphysical consciousness*), and *projected* states.

Para-genetics – Genetics of a human embryo submitted to the influence of *consciential* inheritance from the previous life through the *psychosoma*.

Para-man – *Extraphysical consciousness* having the appearance of a man or projected man. Outworn synonymous expression: *masculine spiritual entity*.

Para-pathology – Pathology of the vehicles of manifestation of *consciousness*, excluding the human body or *soma*.

Para-physiology – Physiology of the vehicles of manifestation of *consciousness*, excluding the human body or *soma*.

Parapsychophysical repercussions – Reactions between 2 vehicles of *consciential* manifestation when they enter into contact with each other. They can be different vehicles of the same *consciousness* or similar vehicles of 2 or more *consciousnesses*. These repercussions can be *intraphysical* and *extraphysical*.

Para-thosene (*para + tho + sen + ene*) – *Thosene* of an *extraphysical consciousness*.

Para-woman – *Extraphysical consciousness* having the appearance of a woman or projected woman. Outworn synonymous expression: *feminine spiritual entity*.

Patho-thosene (*patho + tho + sen + ene*) – Pathological *thosene* or a thosene of *consciential* dementia; *little venial sin*; sick intention; *cerebral rumination*.

Penial aura – *Sex-chakral* energy around the penis, notably when in erection, perceivable by any motivated individual, especially by the sexually excited man.

Penta (*pe + en + ta*) – Multi-dimensional, daily, *personal energetic task*. The individual who performs *penta* receives continuous assistance from the *Helpers* on a long-term basis or for the rest of their life. Popular expression: *passes-to-the-dark*.

Permanent-total-freedom-from-intrusion – Condition of being permanently and totally free of intrusion.

Personal experience – Non-transferable, direct, personal experimentation by an *intraphysical consciousness* who is on his or her evolutionary path.

Personal principles – Package of guiding values and initiatives of *consciential* life, chosen by a *consciousness* through *holomaturity*, multi-dimensionality and day-to-day *cosmoethicality*.

Phenomenon concomitant to CP – That phenomenon occurring, whether within the time-space *continuum* or not, simultaneously with a *conscious projection*, in a spontaneous or unexpected manner.

Physical base – Safe locale, chosen by the *intraphysical consciousness* to leave his or her *soma* in repose while consciously projected to another, exterior, *consciential* dimension; *duodrome*. A domiciliary *projectiogenic holothosene*. Has a direct relation to: energetically sealed bedroom; *penta*; *consciential epicenter*; *extraphysical clinic*; *projectarium*; *precognitarium*; *retrocognitarium*.

Phyto-thosene (*phyto* + *tho* + *sen* + *ene*) – The rudimentary *thosene* of a plant; the *lexical unit* of a plant, according to *Conscientiology*.

Podo-soma (*podo* + *soma*) – The *soma* when considered specifically in regards to the application of feet or foot-related work, as in the case of a soccer player.

Poly-karma (*poly* + *karma*) – Principle of cause and effect active in evolution of *consciousness*, when centered in an experience of cosmic *maxi-fraternity*, beyond *ego-karma* and *group-karma*.

Poly-karmality – Qualities of the *poly-karmic* manifestations of *consciousness*.

Post-somatic intermission – A *consciousness'* extraphysical period immediately following its *somatic* deactivation.

Precognitarium – Physical base technically prepared for the production of precognitive CPs.

Pre-couple – Preliminary stage in human sexuality within *intraphysical society*; flirting.

Pre-intraphysical mandate – *Existential program* for human life, planned before the *intraphysical* rebirth of a *consciousness*; *existential program*.

Pre-kundalini – Secondary chakra at the sole of the foot. There are 2 *pre-kundalini* chakras in the *holosoma* of an *intraphysical consciousness* – one on the bottom of each foot. This is a *conscientiological* expression.

Pre-serenissimus – *Intraphysical* or *extraphysical consciousness* who does not yet live a life of lucid *serenism* (see *Homo sapiens serenissimus*).

Pre-somatic intermission – A *consciousness'* *extraphysical* period immediately preceding its *intraphysical* rebirth.

Primo-thosene (*primo* + *tho* + *sen* + *ene*) – Same as the *First Cause of the universe*; the first compound thought. This term has no plural form.

Projectarium – *Physical base* technically prepared for the production of consciousness projections.

Projectiography – Technical study of *projectiological* records.

Projectiology (Latin: *projectio*, projection; Greek: *logos*, treatise) – Science that studies *projection of consciousness* and its effects, as well as the projection of *consciential energies* outside the *holosoma*.

Projectiotherapy – Science of prevention and therapies derived from *projectiological* research and techniques.

Projective phenomenon – A specific psychic occurrence within the scope of *projectiological* research.

Projective recess – Existential phase of an *intraphysical consciousness* characterized by a spontaneous cessation – almost always temporary –within a sequence of intensive lucid projective experiences.

Proto-thosene (*proto* + *tho* + *sen* + *ene*) – More rudimentary *thosene;* same as *phyto-thosene* or *hypo-thosene.*

Psychic accident – Physical or psychological disturbance generated through energetic, *interconsciential* or pathological influences, generally having an *extraphysical* or multi-dimensional origin.

Psychic signs – Self-aware existence, identification and employment of energetic, animic, psychic and personal signs that all *intraphysical consciousnesses* possess.

Psychosoma (Greek: *psyche*, soul; *soma*, body) – Emotional para-body of *consciousness*; the *objective body* of *intraphysical consciousness*.

Psychosomatic intrusion – Invasion of a *consciousness* by another through emotionality, or through the *psychosoma*.

Rethosene (*re* + *tho* + *sen* + *ene*) – Repeated thosene. Same as *monothosene* or fixed idea.

Retrocognitarium – *Physical base* technically prepared for the production of *retrocognitive conscious projections (CPs)*.

Retrocognition (Latin: *retro*, back; *cognoscere*, to know) – Perceptive capacity whereby an *intraphysical consciousness* knows facts, scenes forms, objects, successes and experiences that pertain to a time in the distant past. These issues commonly have to do with his or her *holo-memory*.

Retrothosene (*retro* + *tho* + *sen* + *ene*) – *Thosene* specifically related to *self-retrocognitions*; same as the engram of mnemotechnics; the *unit of measurement* of *retrocognitions*, according to *Conscientiometry*.

Self-conscientiality – Quality of level of self-knowledge of a *consciousness;* mega-knowledge.

Self-projection – The intentional or willful departure of the *intraphysical consciousness* to another *consciential* dimension, utilizing the *psychosoma* or the *mentalsoma*.

Self-relay – Self-relay is the advanced condition in which a more lucid consciousness evolves by consecutively interweaving various intraphysical existences together.

Self-thosene (*self* + *tho* + *sen* + *ene*) – *Thosene* of the *consciousness* itself.

Self-unrelenting – *Intraphysical consciousness* who does not pardon his or her own errors or omissions, in order to eliminate conscious self-corruption. This positive state supports the likewise healthy condition of *hetero*-forgiver, a sincere *universal forgiver* of all beings forever – *a basic principle of mega-brotherhood*.

Semi-conscious projection (SCP) – Dream experience in which a projected *intraphysical consciousness* finds him or herself lucid to some degree, in a confused manner; lucid dream. It is not an ideal *projection of consciousness*.

Sene (*sen + ene*) – Sentiment and *consciential energy*.

Serenissimus – Popular name for *Homo sapiens serenissimus*.

Seriality – Quality of *consciousness* submitted to *existential seriation* (rebirth cycle*)*.

Sex-chakra (*sex + chakra*) – Root or *sexual chakra of human consciousness*. Ancient expression related to the *consciential energy* of this chakra: *kundalini* (*serpentine fire*).

Sex-soma (*sex + soma*) – The *soma* when considered specifically in relation to its sex.

Sex-somatics – Study of the *soma,* specifically in regards to its sex or sex-soma and its relationship to *intraphysical consciousness*, whether man or woman.

Sex-thosene (*sex + tho + sen + ene*) – Sexual fantasy; the *unit of measurement* of mental adultery, according to *Conscientiometry.*

Soma – Human body; body of an individual in the *Animal* kingdom, *Chordata* phylum, *Mammiferous* class, *Primates* order, *Hominidae* family, *Homo* genus, and *Homo sapiens* species – being the most elevated level of animal on this planet; the most rudimentary vehicle of the *holosoma* of *human consciousness*, regardless of its appearance.

Spermatic intrusion – Introduction of a man's sperm into a woman's *sex-soma* during the sex act.

Strong trait – Strong point or trait of the personality of an *intraphysical consciousness*; positive component of the structure of one's *consciential* universe that propels the evolution of *consciousness.*

Sub-thosene (*sub + tho + sen + ene*) – *Thosene* charged with *consciential energy* from the *abdominal sub-brain,* most notably energy of the *umbilical-chakra*; the *unit of measurement* of the *abdominal sub-brain,* according to *Conscientiometry.*

Suspended animation – That state in which an *intraphysical consciousness* has temporarily suspended the essential vital functions of its cellular body, later returning to its normal physiological conditions. In certain cases, this occurs without suffering any damage to personal health – the cells surviving in a metabolism of human hibernation.

Sympathetic assimilation – Willful assimilation (absorption) of the *consciential energies* of another *consciousness*, resulting from a degree of openness or rapport with said *consciousness*. Not uncommonly, this condition is accompanied by the decodification of a set of another *consciousness*' *thosenes*.

Sympathetic de-assimilation – Cessation of the *sympathetic assimilation* of *consciential energies* through the use of one's will, normally through the installation of a *vibrational state*.

Tachy-thosene (*tachy* + *tho* + *sen* + *ene*) – Rapid thosene, natural to the *tachy-psychic* (quick thinking) *intraphysical consciousness*.

Tele-thosene (*tele* + *tho* + *sen* + *ene*) – Same as *homothosene*.

Theorice (*theor* + *ice*) – Experience of both theory and practice on the part of an *intraphysical* or *extraphysical consciousness*.

Thosen (*tho* + *sen*) – Thought and sentiment.

Thosene (*tho* + *sen* + *ene*) – Practical unit of manifestation of *consciousness*, according to *Conscientiology*, that considers thought or idea (conception), sentiment or emotion, and *consciential energy* as being 3 indissociable elements.

Thosener – Instrument through which *consciousness* manifests its thoughts and acts. In the case of *intraphysical consciousness*, the fundamental thosener is the *soma*.

Thosenic intrusion – Invasion of a *consciousness* upon another by way of the *mentalsoma*.

Thosenity – Quality of one's *thosenic* awareness.

Tri-thanatose – Deactivation and discarding of the *psychosoma* upon the entrance of *Homo sapiens serenissimus* into the condition of *Free Consciousness; third death; third de-soma*.

Umbilical-chakra (*umbilical* + *chakra*) – Chakra located above the navel. Related to the (abdominal) physiology and paraphysiology of *human consciousness*.

Universalism – Set of ideas derived from the universality of the basic laws of nature and the universe. Universalism inevitably becomes the dominant philosophy of consciousness, as a result of our natural evolution; cosmism.

Vehicle of consciousness – Instrument or body whereby *consciousness* manifests in *intraphysicality* (*intraphysical consciousness*) and in the *extraphysical* dimensions (projected individual and *extraphysical consciousness*).

Verbaction (*verb + action*) – Coherent interaction between what is said and done by a *consciousness*; result of one's words being ratified by one's actions.

Vibrational state – Technical condition of maximal dynamization of the *holochakral* energies, through the impulse of will.

Waking non-alignment – Psychic condition in which the *intraphysical projector*, while in the ordinary waking state, perceives that the *psychosoma* is in *non-alignment* or not completely reintegrated with the *soma*. This generates the intensification of psychic perceptions and energetic and psychic phenomena.

Weak trait – Weak point or trait of the personality of an *intraphysical consciousness*; negative component of the structure of one's *consciential* universe that the individual is not yet able to overcome.

Willful intrusion – Invasion of the will of a *consciousness* on another through hetero-suggestion or hetero-hypnosis.

Xenophrenia (Greek: *xenos*, strange; *phrem*, mind) – State of *human consciousness* outside the normal pattern of waking state, induced by physical, physiological, psychological, pharmacological or psychic agents; altered state of *consciousness*.

Xeno-thosene *xeno + tho + sen + ene*) – Meddlesome *thosene* of an *intruder* in the occurrences of *thosenic intrusion*; *mental wedge*; *unit of measurement* of *interconsciential intrusion*, according to *Conscientiometry*.

Zoo-thosene (*zoo + tho + sen + ene*) – *Thosene* of an unaware sub-human animal; *unit of measurement* of a sub-human animal's *consciential* principle, according to *Conscientiometry*.

BIBLIOGRAPHY

1. VIEIRA, Waldo; *Conscienciograma: Técnica de Avaliação da Consciência Integral;* 344 pages; 100 pages of evaluation; 2.000 items; 4 indexes; 11 enumerations; 7 bibliographic references; glossary with 282 terms; 150 abbreviations; alphabetical; 21 x 14 cm.; br.; 1st edition; Rio de Janeiro, RJ, Brazil; Instituto Internacional de Projeciologia; 1996; pages 53, 71, 75, 83, 95, 108, 111, 113, 122, 127, 135, 136, 140, 141, 143, 145, 149, 165, 172, 183, 189, 191, 197, 202, 219, 227, 230. (Editions in Portuguese and Spanish).

2. IDEM; *Penta Manual: Personal Energetic Task;* 138 pages; 34 chapters; 5 bibliographic references; glossary with 282 terms; 147 abbreviations; alphabetical; 21 x 14 cm.; br.; 1st edition; Rio de Janeiro, RJ, Brazil; Instituto Internacional de Projeciologia; 1995; pages 14, 49, 58, 60, 81, 94, 99. (Editions in Portuguese, Spanish and English).

3. IDEM; *Máximas da Conscienciologia;* 164 pages; 150 illustrations; 450 mini-phrases; 10 x 15 cm.; 1st edition; Rio de Janeiro, RJ, Brazil; Instituto Internacional de Projeciologia; 1996; pages 39, 46, 126.

4. IDEM; *Minidefinições Conscienciais;* 164 pages; 150 illustrations; 450 mini-phrases; 10 x 15 cm.; 1st edition; Rio de Janeiro, RJ, Brazil; Instituto Internacional de Projeciologia; 1996; pages 37, 84, 142.

5. IDEM; *Miniglossário da Conscienciologia;* 57 pages; 17 x 11 cm.; Spiral bound; 1st edition; Rio de Janeiro, RJ, Brazil; Instituto Internacional de Projeciologia; 1992; pages 46, 47.

6. IDEM; *Nossa Evolução;* 168 pages; 15 chapters; 6 bibliographic references; glossary with 282 terms; 149 abbreviations; alphabetical; 21 X 14 cm.; br.; 1st edition; Rio de Janeiro, RJ, Brazil; Instituto Internacional de Projeciologia; 1996; pages 41, 59, 60, 63, 70, 86, 106, 136. (Editions in Portuguese and Spanish).

7. IDEM; *O Que é a Conscienciologia;* 180 pages; 100 chapters; 3 bibliographic references; glossary with 280 terms; alphabetical; 21 x 14 cm.; br.; 1st edition; Rio de Janeiro, RJ, Brazil; Instituto Internacional de Projeciologia; 1994; pages 126-128.

8. IDEM; *Projeciologia: Panorama das Experiências da Consciência Fora do Corpo Humano;* XXVIII + 900 pages; 475 chapters; 40 illustrations; 1.907 bibliographic references; glossary with 15 terms; 58 abbreviations; ono.; geo.; alph.; 27 x 18,5 x 5 cm.; enc.; 3rd edition; Londrina; Paraná; Brazil; Livraria e Editora Universalista; 1990; pages 710,711.

9. IDEM; *Projections of the Consciousness: A Diary of Out-of-Body Experiences;* 224 pages; glossary with 25 terms; alph.; 21 x 14 cm.; br.; 4th edition revised; Rio de Janeiro, RJ, Brazil; Instituto Internacional de Projeciologia; 1992; pages 24-26. (Editions in Portuguese, Spanish and English).

10. IDEM; *700 Experimentos da Conscienciologia;* 1058 pgs.; 700 chapters; 300 tests; 8 indexes; 2 tabulations; 600 enumerations; ono.; 5.116 refs.; geo.; glossary with 280 terms; 147 abbreviations; alph.; 28,5 x 21,5 x 7 cm.; enc.; 1st edition; Rio de Janeiro, RJ, Brazil; Instituto Internacional de Projeciologia; 1994; pages 69, 114, 139, 174, 214, 272, 283, 312, 323, 361, 371, 387, 390, 412, 416, 421, 431, 434, 507, 515, 517, 527, 529, 532, 538-540, 567, 579, 583, 585, 599, 604, 609-616, 624, 627, 628, 677, 682, 703, 723, 724, 726, 737, 738.

INDEX

Observation: The numbers listed indicate page numbers. In the cases of there being more than one page number, the one in italic indicates the main reference.

Abortions, 70
Activity, 56
Adoration, 70
Age, *39*, 68
Agenda, 41
Alienation, 74
Anti-city, 53
Anti-cosmoethical, 83
Art, *103*, 124
Artifacts, *87*, 91, 94
Assets, 113
Assistance, 132
Assistentiality, *26*, 113, 139
Authenticity, 13
Average, 42
Banalities, 67
Basement, *56*, 75
Bioenergetics, 47, *99*, 102
Book, 89
Businessperson, 122
Career, *87*, 88
Categories, 12
Causes, 73
Child (ren), *15*, 39, 65
Chronogram, 55
City, 52
Clarification task, 17, *32*, 45, 60, 81, 106
Clauses of existential program, 27, *48*
Code, 18

Coherence, 65
Collections, 14
Competitiveness, *14,* 34
Computer, 29
Cons, 107
Consciential epicenter, *108,* 113, 138
Consciential gestations, *41,* 46
Consciential retailing, *46,* 73, 75
Consciential tri-endowment, 84
Consciential wholesaling, *45,* 46
Conscientiality, *57,* 88
Conscientiocentrism, *40,* 42, 82
Conscientiogram, 30
Conscientiology, *5,* 76
Conscientiometry, *30,* 41
Consolation task, *32,* 73, 75, 118
Constancy, 55
Contemporaneity, 39
Cooperative, 42
Corporatism, 88
Cosmo-ethic, *76,* 83, 95, 117, 119
Cross-roads,
Crutches, 34, 36
Cryogenics, *70,* 71
Deficient, 77
Definitions, *9,* 14, 17, 49, 61, 72, 76, 84, 93, 98, 116, 121, 126, 128-130, 138
Demagogy, 34
De-soma, 15
  Premature de-soma, 121
Destiny, 10
Dictionary, 89
Dietitian, 122
Discernment, 56
Discipline, 56
Discordance,
Dissidence, 66
Dissident, 76
Dogmatic, 34
Driver, 122

Duo, 90
Ectopia, 83
Education, 77
Egocentrism, 81
Ego-karmality, *21*, 83
Ego-karmic existential mini-program,
Emergency, 99
Emotionality,
Endorphin, 51
Energetic springtime, 100
Energy, 98
Eunuch, 50
Evolution, *19*, 38, 138
Evolutionality, *13*, 36
Evolutionary pre-requisites, 133
Evolutionologist, *13*, 26, 130
Existential anti-program, *61*, 122
Existential completion, 116
Existential incompletism, 121
Existential inversion, *41*, 44, 94
Existential maxi-program, 130
Existential mini-moratorium, 129
Existential mini-program, 13, *14*, 117
Existential moratorium, 128
Existential multi-completism, 126
Existential multi-completist, 126
Existential program test, 23
Existential program, 5, *9*
Existential recycling, *41*, 43, 73, 75
Existential robotization, *40*, 61, 85
Existential seriation, *48*, 109
Experience, 118
Extraphysical clinic, 47
Extraphysical consciousness, *18*, 67, 105
Extraphysical euphoria, 15, *116*
Extraphysical melancholy, 71, *123*
Fact (s), *59*, 68
Faction producing doctrines, 94
Fame, 68
Feminism, 50

Field, *53*, 68
Formula of receipt-reciprocation, 29
Formula of traits, 29
Formulas, 28
Friendship, *76*, 77
Future, 110
Geography, 52
Gold, 68
Group of existential invertors, 44
Group of existential recyclers, 43
Groupal existential moratorium, 131
Groupal existential program, 13, 18, 45
Groupal gestations, 46
Groupality, *15*, 18, 42, 43, 83
Group-karmality, *21*, 32
Gyno-soma, 49
Health, *27*, 99
Helpers, *19*, 47, 48
Hetero-scrutiny, *29*, 87, 90
Heuristic, 94
History, 11
Holo-chakra, 98
Holo-karmality, 12
Holo-maturity, *36*, 60, 68, 77
Holo-thosene, 65
Home, 52
Hormones, 51
Human longevity, 114
Hyperacuity, 59
Hypocrisy, 33
Hypomnesia syndrome, 64
Identification of personal existential program, 26
Immaturity, 33
Inculcation, 34
Indecision, 68
Individual dissidence, 79
Infancy, 65, *107*
Institute, *42*, 85
Instruments for the existential project, 38
Intellectuality, 47

Intelligences, *39,* 86
Inter-cooperation, 44
Intraphysical consciousness, 27
Intraphysical euphoria, 116
Intraphysical recycling, *41,* 43
Intraphysical society, 42
Intrudability, *62,* 83
Intuition, *40,* 42, 79
Joint dissidence, 79
Laboratories, 52
Level,
Library, 89
Limit, 26
Link (bond), 42
Losses,
Love, *18,* 44
Lung specialist, 122
Macro-soma, *19,* 45, 118, 119, 131
Macro-somatics, 49
Maintenance, 55
Man, *49,* 69
Manipulation,
Marathons, 51
Maxi-dissidence, 80
Maxi-universalism, 36
Mega-fraternity, *11,* 39, 45
Menopause, 49
Mentalsoma, *50,* 122
Mentalsomatics, 35, 38, *93*
Mini-dissidence, 80, *81*
Mini-dissident, 82
Mini-mechanism, *81,* 83
Minute, 106
Modernity, 52
Money, 27
Mono-endowments, 85
Mutilation of the mentalsoma, 124
Nature, 53
Neophilia, *54,* 65
Neophobia, *66,* 73, 131

Neo-synapse, 90
Non-intrudability, *95,* 96
Novelty,
Numbness, 34
Object, 5
Obligations, 31
Omissions, *31,* 80
Orthodoxy, 34
Paradigms,
Para-genetics, *30,* 62, 137
Para-pathology, 123
Para-perceptions, 102
Parapsychism, 102
Parapsychologists, 67
Para-scars, *30,* 123
Past-present, 107
Pending, 31
Penta, 41, 46, 60, *94*-96, 100, 113, 139
Percentage,
Perfectionism, *66,* 67
Periods, 50
Permanently-totally-intrusion-free, 13
Permanent-total-freedom-from-intrusion, 11, 59, 126, *138*
Personal,
Phases, 46
Platform,
Politics, 122
Polyglotism, *87,*89
Poly-karma, 12
Poly-karmality, *17,* 32, 57, 83, 130
Practice, 61
Precognition, 109
Present-future, 107
Primary goals,
Priorities, 14
Prioritization, 12
Prison, 49
Problem, 133
Procreation, 73
Professionality, 47

Project, 55
Promiscuity, 70
Psychiatry, 122
Questions, *25,* 119, 126
Question-tests, *123,* 127
Readings, 89
Realization, *31,* 55
Recycling, 31
Reference book, 91
Re-soma, 70
Scars, 30
Science, *38,* 59, 88, 102
Seated-on-the-fence, *16,* 66
Secondary goals,
Self- complacency, 64
Self-awareness, 26
Self-corruption, *59,* 60, 62, 82
Self-discipline, 27
Self-disorganization, 122
Self-education, *87,* 89
Self-mastery, *30,* 37
Self-mimicry, *16,* 67, 74, 109
Self-organization, *114,* 127, 136
Self-scrutiny, *35,* 57, 87, 90
Sentiment, 46
Separation,
Sex, 50
Sex-love, 18
Shock of holothosenes, 66
Simplicity, 66
Simul-cognitions,
"Still not it" technique, 59
Stimulus, 38
Strong trait, *29,* 58, 94, 96, 114, 138
Surgeon, 118
Swedenborg syndrome, 81
Synapses, 43
Synonymy, *9,* 14, 17, 49, 61, 72, 76, 84, 88, 116, 121, 126, 128, 130
Task, 32

Technique for the execution of the existential program, 55
Technique, 27
Theorice, *60,* 67, 104
Theory, 61
Thosenity, *77,* 117
Time, *15,* 110
Trinomial rationality-discernment-holo-maturity, 93
Trinomial, 56
Truth, *18,* 36
Types of intelligence, 84
Undertaking,
Universalism, *65,* 66, 96
University, *87,* 88
Urbanite, 52
Vaccination, 10
Variation, 10
Vibrational state, 41, *43,* 95, 138
VS, 41, *43,* 95, 138
Will, 57
Woman, 49
Writer, 118
Writing, *102,* 123
Youths, 91

International Institute of Projectiology and Conscientiology

The International Institute of Projectiology and Conscientiology (IIPC) is a non-profit institution of research and education, or laboratory-school, that has been dedicated to the study of consciousness and its bioenergetic and projective (out-of-body) manifestations since its foundation in 1988.

Having the objective of disseminating its *conscientiology* and *projectiology* research findings to researchers and the public, IIPC has published various books and has developed a regular program of educational activities, conferences, courses, lectures, workshops and other activities at all of its offices. Groups of foreigners regularly visit the Institute, which is able to give its courses in Portuguese, English and Spanish.

IIPC Statistics

Offices:
- Main office in Rio de Janeiro
- 68 national and international offices: Alfenas, Americana, Aracaju, Arapiraca, Avare, *Barcelona,* Belem, Belo Horizonte, Blumenau, Brasília, *Buenos Aires,* Campo Grande, *Caracas,* Cascavel, Criciúma, Cuiabá, Curitiba, Feira de Santana, Florianópolis, Fortaleza, Iguacu Falls, Goiania, Guaira, Guarapuava, Guaratingueta, Ijui, Itajuba, Ji-Parana, Joinville, João Pessoa, Jundiaí, Lambari, *Lisbon, London,* Londrina, Maceió, Manaus, Maringá, Mogi das Cruzes, Mogi-Guaçu, Montes Claros, *Miami,* Natal, Niteroi, *New York,* Novo Hamburgo, Osasco, *Ottawa,* Pelotas, Pirassununga, Porto Alegre, Porto Velho, Recife, Riberão Preto, Rio Branco, Salvador, Santos, São Bernardo do Campo, São José dos Campos, São Paulo, São Pedro D'Aldeia, São Vicente, Torres, Três Pontas, Vila Mariana, Vitória.

47 Research Groups in 7 Areas:
- Computer Science
- Conscientiological Intraphysical Society

- Conscientiotherapy
- Existential Inversion
- Existential Recycling
- Leading-edge Research
- Independent Research

Mailing List:
- 87,085 Individuals
- 1,275 Institutions

Educational activities. IIPC has developed two types of courses:

Regular courses include those with and without prerequisite. The five stages (in English) with prerequisite provide information on the history, ideas and research results achieved over the last 30 years in the field of Conscientiology and Projectiology, as well as teaching and allowing practice with various techniques. Non-prerequisite courses focus on specific themes in the area of Conscientiology and Projectiology.

Extracurricular courses, also without prerequisite, are a result of the research performed by IIPC teachers in diverse fields of study in conventional science, as well as Conscientiology and Projectiology, with a consciential approach. Human sexuality, existential inversion and penta (personal energetic task) are among the themes addressed.

Lectures, open to the public and free of charge, are held regularly at all IIPC offices.

IIPC International Offices

Buenos Aires, Argentina
Since 1992, the Buenos Aires office has operated as a base serving to integrate Conscientiology and Projectiology in South American countries, as well as the rest of Latin America. It is giving support for the implantation of the Caracas Office.

Lisbon, Portugal
The Lisbon office has been offering its activities since 1994 and maintains contact with researchers and organizations in France and Italy.

London, UK
The London office gives the CDP on a regular basis and maintains contact with the Society for Psychical Research (SPR) – the mother organization of the ASPR.

Ottawa, Canada
The newly activated Ottawa office holds public lectures and offers the CDP on a regular basis.

New York & Miami, USA
The New York and Miami offices have been giving the IIPC Consciousness Development Program (CDP) in English since 1994. The New York office currently offers the CDP in New York, New Jersey and Massachusetts. It maintains contact with various institutions, including the American Society for Psychical Research (ASPR), one of the oldest and most important parapsychology research institutions in the world. The Miami office, established in 1994, holds its activities in both English and Spanish.

Having the multi-dimensional and cosmoethical objective of catalyzing the holomaturity of more aware pre-serenissimus, IIPC is open to all researchers who are motivated to collaborate with its advanced proposals. If you are interested in working as a mini-piece of the maxi-mechanism of conscientiality, contact the IIPC office closest to you.

Headquarters

Rio de Janeiro, Brazil
Rua Visconde de Pirajá, 572 / 6° andar
Rio de Janeiro, RJ 22410-002, Brazil
Tel.:(021) 512-4735 Fax:(021) 512-9229
E-mail: iipc@ax.ibase.org.br

CEAEC - Centro de Altos Estudos da Consciência:
Caixa Postal 1027 - Centro - Foz do Iguaçu
PR - CEP 85851-000
Fone / Fax (045) 525. 2652
E-mail – ceaec@foznet.com.br

Homepages:
http://www.iipc.org.br
http://www.foznet.com.br/ceaec
http://members.aol.com/iipnyusa/iipc.htm

International Offices

Buenos Aires, Argentina
Calle Azcuenaga, 797/10°A
Pc. Buenos Aires 1029 Argentina
Tel./fax: (541) 951-5048
E-mail: iipcbsas@interactive.com

Lisbon, Portugal
Rua Pascoal de Melo, 84 - 1° Esq. sl.11
Lisbon 1000 - Portugal
Tel: (511) 353-6339
E-mail: iipclxpt@mail.telepac.pt

London, UK
45 Great Cumberland Pl. – London W1H 7LH
E-mail: London@iipc.org
Web: www.iipc.org
Phone: +44 (0)20 7723-0544

Miami, USA
7800 S.W. 57 Ave., Suite 207D
South Miami, FL 33143, USA
Tel.: (305) 668-4668 Fax: (305) 668-4663
E-mail: iipcflusa@aol.com

New York, USA
2O E. 49 St., Ste. 2F, New York, NY 10017
Tel./fax: (718) 721-6257
E-mail: iipcnyusa@aol.com

Ottawa, Canada
60 Laurie Court
Kanata, ONT K2L 1S4 Canada
Tel./fax: (613) 831-4483
E-mail: iipcotwca@cyberus.ca

For information on other offices, contact IIPC's main office.

CONSCIENTIOLOGICAL COMPLEX

The International Institute of Projectiology and Conscientiology (IIPC) is implanting a *CONSCIENTIOLOGICAL COMPLEX* in Iguacu Falls, Paraná, Brazil. This will be a center for work, research, residence and *conscientiological* assistance. An area of 24.2 acres (9.68 hectares) is being developed. This area is next to natural foliage and a stream. Its objective is the implantation of a center for the research and dissemination of the worthy ideas of *conscientiology* and *projectiology*, as a type of *conscientiological* district. One of the characteristics of the area of Iguacu Falls is its great quantity of high quality *immanent energy* – a fact which greatly aids in the *holothosene* of this future district. Iguacu Falls also stands out due to its proximity to Argentina and Paraguay. It is the second largest touristic area in Brazil and, for this reason, receives a great quantity of visitors from the world over. These characteristics of Iguacu Falls contribute towards the globalization of the *clarification task* – promoted by IIPC. The *Conscientiological Complex* is composed of the following facets:

Center for Higher Studies of Consciousness

The *Center for Higher Studies of Consciousness* is the Complex's research center. Its objective is to promote social benefits through educational, scientific, technological, commercial and ethical solutions, accelerating *group evolution*.

The following spaces are planned:

- The **Projectarium** is a building that combines all ideal elements characteristic for the engendering of lucid projection of consciousness.

- The **Holo-archive** is a display facility for the permanent exposition of artifacts of knowledge that will be distributed among 100 stands and will include space for Dr. Vieira's library, which includes 30,000 volumes, being one of the most specialized in the world on subjects regarding projection of consciousness.

- **Immersion Courses**, or Extension in Conscientiology/Projectiology 1 (ECP1) and Extension in Conscientiology/Projectiology 2 (ECP2), that are given over weekends and require exclusive accommodations.

- **Conscientiotherapy (consciousness therapy) Clinic**, for public consultations.

- **Event Pavilion** – a large building in which all IIPC activities are concentrated, such as congresses, forums, symposiums, conferences workshops, assemblies, video and film projections, etc.

- **Lodging for researchers** – a hotel service for those engaged in the activities of the Center.

- **Publishing House** and **Print Shop** for the literary production of the Complex and IIPC.

- **Conscientiological School**, allowing individuals to work according to cosmoethical and universalist principles.

- **Environmental Recuperation** of the entire area, including a wooded area comprising 20% of the total area of the Center. This area will be devoted to planting fruit-bearing, medicinal and bird-attracting plants, forest recuperation and landscaping with native plant species.

- **Conscientiological Administration** – a building that would join the teams that will administrate the Complex. These teams will also offer administrative assistance to interested professional companies.

The Center's plans include innovative principles, aiming to increase the researchers' effectiveness, focusing on *mentalsomatics*. The *holo-archive* is the central building of this project.

Conscientiological Residential Complex. Adapted to the profile of the *conscientiology/projectiology* researcher, this residential complex has a tone of multi-dimensional architecture that takes *holosomatic* and *multi-dimensional* aspects into consideration. It is planned with the intention of creating a residential complex similar to advanced *extraphysical communities*, having a sensible philosophy and space planning. The residents will have areas for performing *penta*, research, maintaining a library, etc. This complex will catalyze group and individual existential programs and allow the residents to work in an environment of heightened conviviality. This tends to predispose those individuals engaged in this mega-challenge to an inevitably greater self-knowledge, and an unprecedented self-confrontation within a group of persons interested in evolution of consciousness.

Service Shopping Center. In order to completely meet the needs of the Complex's researchers, the service shopping center was conceived within the philosophical principles of *conscientiology*. Its aim is to bring together *conscientiological* companies and professionals who will offer *cosmoethical* services to the general public.